READING THE
NEW TESTAMENT TODAY

Reading the
New Testament Today

An Introduction to New Testament Study

by

Brian E. Beck

JOHN KNOX PRESS
ATLANTA

First published in Great Britain in 1977 by Lutterworth Press. The John Knox Press edition is published by arrangement with Lutterworth Press.

Library of Congress Cataloging in Publication Data

Beck, Brian E.   1933-
    Reading the New Testament today.

    Includes bibliographical references and index.
    1. Bible. N.T.—Study.   2. Lord's prayer.
I. Title.
BS2530.B4   1978   225'.07   78-14420
ISBN 0-8042-0391-1

© copyright Brian E. Beck 1978
Printed in the United States of America
John Knox Press
Atlanta, Georgia

For my parents

Contents

Foreword

This is a book for beginners with serious intentions. It is about approaches and methods, and the reasons for them. By way of illustration it touches on some of the problems of interpretation in the New Testament and gives examples of the way they are dealt with; it does not pretend to treat them exhaustively or to offer a comprehensive survey. For this the reader is referred to the bibliography on page 156. But it does aim to help the student find his way among the more technical works with some sense of perspective, understanding what he is about and how each aspect of his study contributes to the whole. I have tried to take nothing for granted beyond an ordinary familiarity with the New Testament, and to avoid technical terms unless explained.

The scholar on the other hand will find no surprises here. Although the absence of footnotes has ruled out detailed acknowledgement, I offer nothing I have not received, and it will be apparent on every page what I have read (and failed to read). In any case an introductory book should not be a repository of untried innovations.

My thanks are due to many: to those who have urged me on, in particular Professor C. F. D. Moule, generous as always in counsel and encouragement; to the Lutterworth Press for their kindness; and to my typists, Julia Maclagan and Rosalind Cooper. Without them all this book would not have seen the day.

Brian E. Beck
Cambridge 1977

Introduction

Twenty years ago a friend gave me his views on the study of the New Testament, upon which I had just embarked. He recalled his own student days, and in particular the emphatic way in which his New Testament teacher (a distinguished scholar of the time) had rejected as quite impossible a point of view on the gospel of Mark which by the time of our conversation had come to be very widely accepted. Why pay any attention to the scholars, he asked? We may safely leave them to carry on their learned conversations among themselves, for they are sure to come round in the end to the common-sense views which ordinary people have always held. His question, and the assumption behind it, are still evident today, not only in the attacks of critics but, most significantly, in the way in which even those who are aware of the findings of scholarship often ignore them in preaching, teaching and private reading. This book is an attempt to provide a reply; to justify, both for the would-be student and for the general reader, the enterprise of New Testament scholarship as it is carried on today.

Even those who avoid the cynicism of my friend will probably share his frustration. The first encounter with serious textbooks can bring confusion and disillusionment. The disciplines demanded of the student and the conclusions to which he is invited to come are often very different from what he had expected. For many, scholarship seems to make the New Testament more remote than ever. Instead of making its pages more intelligible, it appears to remove them to a more distant and inaccessible world, describable only in barbarous technical terms (*eschatological, kerygmatic, traditio-historical* and the like) whose relevance to the twentieth century is difficult to discern. Scholars seem to be preoccupied with questions which ordinary people never think of asking, and to be incapable of giving a straight answer to the questions they do ask.

Remoteness is not the only problem. Scholars appear to display a dogmatism in their assertions which is unwarrantable

1

in view of the way in which they frequently disagree among themselves. The beginner may be excused for thinking that no question is settled and no judgement endorsed by all those entitled to pronounce upon it. When the experts disagree, how may the uninitiated venture an opinion? Should he not, like my friend, turn his back on the subject altogether; or if he has already embarked on his course and has an essay to turn in next day, what more can he do (sitting on the fence not being an option) than merely adopt whichever point of view coincides with his own prejudices? To begin study of the New Testament seems to many students to forsake knowledge for ignorance and assurance for sheer confusion: the opposite of what one normally expects from the attempt to learn.

What makes it all so much more difficult is that most of those who wish to study a part of the Bible have far more invested in it than in other literature. They are likely to regard it as a supreme source of authoritative teaching about belief and behaviour. They will be accustomed to listen to readings from it during worship in church, and turn to it for devotional purposes in private prayer. The basic pattern of their lives and the chief reference points in their understanding of the world about them may be derived from it. They probably have particular passages which provide resources for them in times of stress. This factor differentiates biblical study from other disciplines. Religion necessarily has a conservative quality, partly because one of its functions in life is to provide a sense of security. Hence while people vary in their ability to make adjustments to their faith, very few can cope with major changes, particularly in later life. The more deeply the faith is held and the more completely life is built upon it, the more difficult it will be to accommodate shifts of perspective in it. So if any of the foundations are disturbed, the whole edifice will be threatened. The substitution of a strange, less evocative translation of a verse for a familiar and loved one, and still more the suggestion that things in the Bible are not actually what they seem (e.g. that there may be a 'rational' explanation for the crossing of the Red Sea or, more radically, that the tomb of Jesus was never found empty) are bound to seem threatening. Some, accepting the judgements which scholars make, may conclude that the edifice of faith is insupportable and better abandoned altogether. Others

2

will resist with vehemence the whole enterprise of biblical study. For them, every claim which scholars make is more outrageous than the last, and it is best to have no dealings with them at all.

In any case, it may be asked, why should the results of biblical study be so different now from what they have been in the past? For centuries the attempt to learn more about the Bible was constructive and edifying. Readers of commentaries felt they were drawing water from deep wells, preachers discovering in them material for sermons, and the ordinary Christian finding his reading of the Bible illuminated and his devotional life strengthened. Why should the Bible now become a book full of problems and unresolved difficulties, a challenge rather than a support for faith? Thus the work of modern scholars can easily appear in the guise of a latter-day unbelieving assault upon convictions which have stood the test of time. Why can we not be satisfied today with an attitude to the Bible which has satisfied our predecessors for nineteen centuries?

These are the questions which we shall attempt to answer in this book. They apply of course to the whole Bible, but our concern here will be with the New Testament. In order to answer them it will be necessary to show, as far as possible in non-technical terms, what New Testament scholarship is about, its aims and methods, and some of its results. It will be shown that there is some truth in the objections we have mentioned. In some respects it is true that New Testament scholarship is remote; it does not offer unanimous answers to every question; it does challenge some current conceptions of Christian faith; it is a relatively modern phenomenon. We shall try to show why this should be so, but we shall also show that the objections are largely based on a misunderstanding of what scholars are doing and the reasons for their work, and that it is a misrepresentation to suggest that the results of the last two hundred years of study carried out by scholars in many countries have been only negative and destructive. In many ways our understanding of New Testament times, of Jesus himself, and of the meaning of the documents in their original setting and their potential significance for our own times have been immeasurably enhanced. It is hoped that the following pages, while providing an outline guide to some of the complexities of New Testament study, will also illustrate some of its many positive gains.

1. Asking Questions

It is not surprising that when the New English Bible New Testament was first published in 1961 it aroused controversy as well as interest. Because of the wide publicity it received, it came to the notice of many who had been unaware of the numerous other versions published in the previous hundred years, and who knew only the Authorized Version of 1611. Some found it shocking that the words of the Bible could be altered. It seemed that the translators were daring to tamper with words which had the sanction of divine revelation. For some time the focus of the protest was the Lord's Prayer, which one newspaper had featured on its front page on publication day. Here, apparently, were words given by Jesus himself which the translators had now altered. What the objectors did not realize was that the same protest could have been made when the Authorized Version was published three hundred and fifty years before.

The Lord's Prayer provides a convenient starting point for our study of the New Testament because it raises a surprising number of the questions with which modern scholarship is concerned. At this stage we shall be more concerned with showing what these questions are; later in the book we shall return to the prayer to see where our enquiries have led us. Five versions of the Lord's Prayer are set out on page 6. The form in which most English speaking people learn it is given in column A. Custom varies in certain churches over the use or omission of lines 12 to 14, but most people can recite it in the fuller form. It was no doubt this version that the objectors had in mind in 1961.

It is an odd fact that, contrary to what most people assume, this version cannot be found in any Bible. It seems to have made its first appearance in the first edition of the Book of Common Prayer in 1549 as the form to be used in Morning and Evening Prayer and Holy Communion. At that stage it lacked the last three lines, which were added in 1662. It did not correspond

5

THE LORD'S PRAYER

	A THE BOOK OF COMMON PRAYER (1549 & 1662)	B AUTHORIZED VERSION (1611) Matthew 6:9-13	C AUTHORIZED VERSION (1611) Luke 11:2-4	D NEW ENGLISH BIBLE (1961) Matthew 6:9-13	E NEW ENGLISH BIBLE (1961) Luke 11:2-4
		After this manner therefore pray ye:	And he said unto them, When ye pray, say,	This is how you should pray:	He answered, When you pray, say,
1.	Our Father,	Our Father	Our Father	Our Father	Father,
2.	which art in heaven,	which art in heaven,	which art in heaven,	in heaven,	
3.	Hallowed be thy Name.	Hallowed be thy name.	Hallowed be thy name.	Thy name be hallowed;	thy name be hallowed;
4.	Thy kingdom come.	Thy kingdom come.	Thy kingdom come.	Thy kingdom come,	Thy kingdom come.
5.	Thy will be done,	Thy will be done,	Thy will be done,	Thy will be done,	
6.	in earth as it is in heaven.	in earth, as it is in heaven.	as in heaven, so in earth.	On earth as in heaven.	
7.	Give us this day our daily bread.	Give us this day our daily bread.	Give us day by day our daily bread.	Give us today our daily bread.	Give us each day our daily bread.
8.	And forgive us our trespasses,	And forgive us our debts,	And forgive us our sins;	Forgive us the wrong we have done,	And forgive us our sins,
9.	As we forgive them that trespass against us.	as we forgive our debtors.	for we also forgive every one that is indebted to us.	As we have forgiven those who have wronged us.	For we too forgive all who have done us wrong.
10.	And lead us not into temptation;	And lead us not into temptation,	And lead us not into temptation;	And do not bring us to the test,	And do not bring us to the test.
11.	But deliver us from evil:	but deliver us from evil:	but deliver us from evil.	But save us from the evil one.	
12.	For thine is the kingdom,	For thine is the kingdom,			
13.	The power, and the glory,	and the power, and the glory,			
14.	For ever and ever. Amen.	for ever. Amen.			

exactly to any of the versions in the many translations of the
Bible made at that period; its closest predecessor was to be
found in another book of prayer, *King Henry's Primer* (1545),
from which it differs in one line. It was an independent translation, designed for use in worship and already familiar for sixty
years when the Authorized Version appeared.

In the Bible itself the Lord's Prayer occurs in two places,
Matthew 6: 9-13 and Luke 11: 2-4. The Authorized Version
does not follow the familiar wording exactly in either passage.
The version in Matthew (column B) is the nearer; it has the
longer form, including lines 12–14, but differs in lines 8 and 9
(*debts* and *debtors*) and, less markedly, in lines 13 (*and the power*)
and 14 (*for ever*). In Luke (column C) the differences are more
striking: in line 6 (*as in heaven, so in earth*), line 7 (*day by day*),
line 8 (*sins*) and almost the whole of line 9. Lines 12–14 are
missing.

Thus those who objected to 'altering the Lord's Prayer' in
1961 had overlooked the fact that there were already two other
versions of the prayer, which they must often have heard read
in church; the translators in 1961 could not be accused of
tampering with it any more than their predecessors in 1611.
The more naïve objectors indeed appear to have forgotten – or
never even realized – that English is not the language of the
Bible. What we have are translations. Nevertheless they had a
point. In some places the New English Bible version (columns
D and E) was so different in both gospels that it was natural to
ask whether the meaning had not been changed. Does *do not
bring us to the test* (line 10) mean the same as *lead us not into
temptation*?

The most striking differences, however, relate to length.
There is a difference in this respect between columns B and C;
it is greater between D and E, and most remarkable when
column E is compared with A. In the new translation neither
gospel contains lines 12 to 14, although a footnote in Matthew
explains that 'some witnesses' add it. In Luke line 1 consists of
the one word *Father*, and lines 2, 5, 6 and 11 are also omitted,
footnotes again explaining that 'some witnesses' add the omitted
portions.

The Authorized Version had also had marginal notes, although they often pass unnoticed today because they are

included among references to parallel passages, or in some editions are not printed at all. Occasionally such a note relates to an alternative reading found by the translators in some copies in the original language, but for the most part they offer an alternative translation of a word or a fuller explanation of its meaning. One such note occurs in the Lord's Prayer in Luke where *for the day* is suggested instead of *day by day*. The New English Bible footnotes thus follow a well established tradition, although they are more clearly set out and, in connexion with the Lord's Prayer at least, more numerous.

Some of the footnotes are concerned with alternative translations (*our bread for the morrow* in place of *our daily bread*), while the others point to variations in the content and length of the prayer. In addition to those already mentioned, a note in Luke informs us that instead of *thy kingdom come* 'one witness reads *thy kingdom come upon us*', and 'some others have *thy Holy Spirit come upon us and cleanse us*'. It seems that the New English Bible translators were in places much more uncertain than their predecessors not only what the correct translation should be, but even what had to be translated. In one respect they became even less certain as time went on, for when the complete Bible was published and the New Testament revised in 1970, they added a further footnote in both gospels, offering the traditional translation *from evil* (line 11) as an alternative to *from the evil one* which they had thought satisfactory nine years earlier.

In part all this is due to the difficulties presented by the task of translation. Those who have had no experience of translation from a foreign language into English often assume the process to be analogous to the conversion of an algebraic formula into an arithmetical expression. If we are told that $x = 2$, $y = 3$ and $z = 5$ we know that the formula xyz can be converted to $2 \times 3 \times 5$, and that other formulae involving these letters can be similarly converted, because the value of the letters remains constant. So, it may be assumed, the sentence *the boy kicks the dog* can be converted into another language simply by substituting the appropriate foreign word for each English one. In the case of some languages and some very simple sentences, this may sometimes appear to be the case. The fact is, however, that a word rarely has a precise counterpart in another language.

An English word may generally coincide in meaning with its foreign equivalent but in certain contexts have a special significance which the foreign word cannot have (compare *I pinched my sister* with *I pinched a pound from the till!*). One language may be rich in synonyms where the other has only one word, or may use a variety of more precise terms covered in the other language by a more general expression (compare the many devotional addresses based on the fact that Greek has three words for *love*, referring to family affection, sexual desire, and God's saving compassion, which the English Christian is urged carefully to distinguish). In addition, languages frequently differ in structure, that is, in the basic method of expressing ideas. Thus many languages are able to express *the boy kicks the dog* without needing any word for *the*. On the other hand, *boy, kick* and *dog* may have to be arranged in a different order from English. Indeed, the order of words may not matter at all, the relationship between them being indicated by some other device, such as a modification of some sort, similar to the *s* which we sometimes add in English to the word *kick*.

All this means that the art of translation is much more subtle than the mere substitution of one word for another. It involves the expression, in a way natural in English, of ideas originally expressed equally naturally in the other language. More than one translation is usually possible, for more is involved than accuracy. Clearly, in the example we have been using *cat* will not do for *dog*, but *the boy strikes the dog with his foot* conveys the same meaning as *the boy kicks the dog*. The question the translator has to answer is which expression is the more natural in English and the more appropriate to the context.

The New English Bible is thus more than a new translation in the sense of turning the New Testament into what is by comparison with the Authorized Version more modern English. It embodies a rather different translation policy. Quite apart from the fact that they were bound by their mandate to keep as closely as possible to previous translations, the Authorized Version translators took a fairly conservative view of their task: wherever they could they kept close to the original structure of the Greek and Hebrew languages from which they were translating. Accordingly, where English usage demanded the insertion of a word with no precise equivalent in the original they printed

9

it in italics. The New English Bible translators on the other hand have attempted to produce not only contemporary English words (*test* for *temptation*) but contemporary ways of speaking (*the wrong we have done* for *our debts*).

A complication is introduced by the fact that in the case of the New Testament the writings we have to translate are very ancient and are written in a language which no one now speaks in the precise form in which it was then used. We know that less than two hundred years after the gospels were written one Greek word in the Lord's Prayer (for which the New English Bible offers the alternatives *daily* or *for the morrow*) was no longer understood even by those for whom Greek was the language of everyday life. This is in spite of the fact, apparently, that they still repeated it when they said the prayer. One wonders what they made of it! The normal way to clarify an obscure word in translating is to ask someone who uses the language daily to explain its meaning, but this way is not open to us because New Testament Greek is a 'dead' language. We have to work out the meaning by other means, and in some cases, like the one before us, we cannot be sure of the answer.

But this does not explain all the facts we have noticed. We are dealing in Matthew and Luke not only with different translations, but with different *versions* of the prayer. Even within each gospel there are questions about the correct reading of the text. The reason for this again lies in the antiquity of the New Testament. The original copies, as they left the hands of the authors, perished long ago and have not exercised the control over subsequent editions which we expect in modern books. In the course of time many errors and variations have crept into the text. In the case of the Lord's Prayer a special factor was doubtless the fact that, as a prayer, it was in constant use, and its wording, modified by repetition, would in turn influence the text of the gospels as copyists wrote what they remembered rather than what they saw before them. The oldest copies of the New Testament we possess differ among themselves, and lacking the originals we have to deduce as scientifically as we can which reading is correct.

Even if we deal with this problem, the question remains, which version did Jesus teach? As we have seen, Matthew and Luke present us with two different versions of the prayer.

They are set in different contexts: in Matthew in the Sermon on the Mount, in Luke as Jesus' reply to a request from his disciples after he had himself been praying. In Matthew the prayer is given as a pattern to be followed ('After this manner pray ye . . .'), in Luke it is an actual prayer to be repeated ('When ye pray, say . . .'). Are we to conclude that Jesus taught the prayer on two occasions? If so, why did he teach two different versions? If on the other hand we conclude that he is more likely to have taught only one form of the prayer, we are still left with the problem of deciding which is the original, or even whether either of them is. For clearly if one gospel contains variations of the version Jesus originally gave, then conceivably both do, and the original prayer would presumably have to be reconstructed somehow from the two versions which have come down to us. Our difficulties therefore involve not only the antiquity of the New Testament, and the attendant problems of translation and correct reading, but also the nature of its contents, in particular the existence of two gospels which do not appear to agree.

Even when we have answered all these questions, we still have not determined which version of the prayer Jesus originally taught. For the Greek versions in the gospel are themselves translations. Whether Jesus knew any Greek at all is a disputed question, but it is generally agreed that most of his teaching was given not in Greek but in a Semitic language, probably the Aramaic dialect which was generally spoken in Galilee. Doubtless the prayer was also taught in this form, so that the strict answer to the question 'What prayer did Jesus actually teach?', if we could arrive at it, would have to be given in Aramaic. Most English speakers, ignorant of Aramaic, would rightly wonder whether that was the answer they were really looking for.

But that is just the question: what kind of answer *are* we looking for when we ask 'what did Jesus teach?' One form of answer certainly would be to try to recover the Aramaic words he uttered, but this would not necessarily tell us what he meant by the words. For the meaning of any statement (in everyday speech at least) is never contained entirely within the words themselves; words do not have precise invariable meanings which can be laid down in advance. They are haunted by associations of ideas which evoke trains of thought and stir the imagination.

11

Their full effect depends upon the fact that speaker and hearer share the same world, the same memories, fears and hopes. We may explain *Boney will get you* correctly enough as *Napoleon Bonaparte will come and punish you*, but have we conveyed the emotions (and nightmares) which the words would have stirred up in the mind of an early nineteenth-century child threatened by his nurse? In order to know what Jesus meant by the words he used, even if we knew what they were and could understand them in the original language, we should need also to know the world in which he lived. We should need to look on life with the eyes of his contemporaries, and feel their hopes and fears, in order to know (for example) whether the words *thy kingdom come* would have filled the hearers with apprehension or made them tingle with joy.

What then does the Lord's Prayer mean? What is the *kingdom* which we pray will *come*? What does it mean for God's *name* to be *hallowed*, and by whom is it to be hallowed? What is our *daily bread* (especially if *daily* is a translator's guess)? What are we to make of *lead us not into temptation*, or the equally obscure *do not bring us to the test*? To ask questions such as these is to embark upon an extensive enquiry into the history, religious ideas, political situation and into every other aspect of the culture of Jesus' time.

Of course we are not aware of this when we say the Lord's Prayer. We automatically supply the words with a meaning of some sort, unless we repeat them as a mere incantation, without thinking about them at all. We are probably more successful with some phrases than with others: *Forgive us our trespasses as we forgive them that trespass against us* is more readily understood than *hallowed be thy name*. But who is to say that the meaning we give to the words is the meaning they were intended to have; or that we have felt their full impact, detected all their overtones? Are we really any better off than those Greeks who repeated the prayer without knowing the meaning of the word we translate as *daily*, and who must have guessed at its meaning in a variety of ways?

The last paragraph brings out the fact that there are different levels of meaning. The aim of speech generally is to convey the speaker's ideas so that they may be shared by the listener. Even in ordinary conversation this is never perfectly achieved, for no

12

one's thoughts are absolutely identical with those of another. Although for all practical purposes we are successful enough, misunderstandings occur sufficiently often to remind us of the difficulties of communication. A listener may invest the speaker's words with a meaning quite different from what was intended. When the communication takes place through the medium of the written word over a long interval of time, the dangers of misunderstanding are greater. Speaker and listener, writer and reader, are now strangers to each other. They belong to different worlds. In extreme cases the result may be that the reader cannot understand the writer at all. He may not possess sufficient clues to the world in which the writer lived to grasp what he is trying to say. What more commonly happens is that, while the reader understands what is written, he remains unaffected by it. He perceives what the words meant to the writer because he is able to project himself back in his imagination into the writer's world, but he cannot see any way to relate them to his own world. He is, as it were, merely overhearing part of a conversation from the past. Only if the writer's meaning can be adjusted somehow to fit the world in which the reader lives will there be a real dialogue in which the reader feels that the writer is addressing him. For the reader to share the writer's ideas some adaptation is needed.

A simple example of such adaptation is the use of a very old cooking recipe. Ingredients may no longer be available in the form prescribed; the cooking appliances and fuel used with them may be different; in consequence the recipe has to be modified if it is to be used at all. A rather better example is the effort which often has to be made in legal circles to interpret the intentions of a benefactor long after his death so that the provisions of his will may still be carried out faithfully in changed circumstances which the benefactor had never envisaged. In all adaptations of this kind we try to express the 'meaning' of a statement in present-day terms. The adaptation must not be arbitrary or irresponsible: we are right to insist that there should be some connexion between the original meaning and the meaning we are now giving the words, for we are trying to say not merely what we *want* the writer's words to mean but what they *must* mean. Nevertheless the result is a meaning never actually envisaged by the author.

The application of all this to the Lord's Prayer is obvious. If we enquire what the words *thy kingdom come* meant for Jesus and his hearers, remembering, on the basis of what we have been considering, that the words probably meant different things to different hearers even at the time, we shall probably conclude that for many of his hearers at least, 'the kingdom of God' suggested a very complex set of ideas. These would include the conviction that God would demonstrate his sovereignty over world events by some dramatic intervention, one which would involve the liberation of the Jews from foreign political power, the restoration of the Jewish monarchy in the person of a king who could trace his family tree back to King David, and the transformation of nature so that deserts became flowering gardens and animals no longer killed each other for food. Above all it would involve the complete reorganization of human relationships so that individuals and nations would for ever after live at peace with each other, serene in the presence of God, in a state of affairs which could best be described as an unending banquet. There is no doubt at all that many of Jesus' contemporaries expected such a divine intervention to occur in their own lifetime, and were actively praying and working for it. We do not now need to go into the question how far Jesus himself shared these ideas. The point is that *if* he did, there will have to be some adaptation of the meaning of the words in order to fit them into the world in which we live, if we are to pray *thy kingdom come* today. We do not share the expectations of first-century Palestinian Jews, and the technological age in which we live and the knowledge we now possess prevent our taking over their world view in its entirety. To ask what these words 'mean' therefore is to ask more than the historical question what they meant when first spoken: it is to ask what meaning they may properly have today. How may we interpret them in our situation in such a way that we preserve some continuity with their original meaning while making them fit, or 'speak to' our world?

Our reflections on the Lord's Prayer have uncovered a surprising number of questions. In fact almost all the major preoccupations of New Testament scholarship have been touched on: problems of translation and of the original text, of the relation between different documents, reconstructing the world

14

in which the New Testament was written, recovering what its central character actually said, and interpreting it both in its original setting and in its application to today. Underlying all these questions has been the assumption that the New Testament contains something worth applying, and that it possesses some kind of authority. All these issues have arisen out of reflection upon a well-known passage. The Lord's Prayer was chosen because of its familiarity, but it would have been possible to produce similar results from many other passages, for when almost any part of the New Testament is read reflectively such questions begin to arise.

It is important to begin in this way if we are to see the study of the New Testament in its proper perspective. In the Introduction we mentioned the complaint that the work of New Testament scholars seems remote. We have now seen how all their central concerns arise naturally out of an intelligent questioning of the text itself. The basic fact of which we must never lose sight is that the Bible as a whole is an ancient book, a collection of documents of which the most recent is nearly nineteen hundred years old. In no other case does one expect writings of such antiquity to have an immediate impact or to present no difficulties of interpretation. The Bible is not an exception. The New Testament, like the Old, demands an answer to the many questions it raises. In the chapters which follow we shall try to show how these questions are tackled.

2. The Original Wording

Nowadays we take the benefits of printing for granted. We expect that all copies of a book will be identical, and that if the author or publisher wishes to introduce changes, he will indicate that he is issuing a revised edition. If, in defiance of this convention, a publisher inserts minor corrections into a reprint without acknowledgement, great irritation can arise, as any teacher knows who has found discrepancies in apparently identical copies of a classroom textbook. Before the invention of printing, however, such discrepancies were common. It is very difficult to copy a long work without any word misspelt or omitted, or any variation in punctuation. When all books were handwritten this kind of error was normal experience and was tolerated more readily.

It has been estimated that we have in our possession today at least thirteen thousand Bibles and Testaments in various languages produced before the adoption of printing. Most of these date from the Middle Ages; the relatively few older copies we possess are often incomplete, and were mostly unknown when the first printed editions of the Bible in Latin and Greek were produced, together with the early translations into English. All of these manuscripts have their individual characteristics.

Very many of the discrepancies are obvious errors of copying which the reader would automatically discount, but some are more serious: the use of an alternative word, variations in word order, the presence of additional words or even whole sentences. Sometimes the result is that the meaning of the passage is radically different. As we saw, examples of such differences occur, at different levels of seriousness, in the Lord's Prayer.

How are we to evaluate these variants? How can we select the version which preserves what the author of a book actually wrote, and – equally important – account for the alternatives? These are the problems with which *textual criticism* deals. It is an attempt to establish scientifically the original wording and account for all the variations which have occurred over the centuries.

Textual criticism is not confined to the New Testament. It is applied to all ancient literature which has survived to us in manuscript form; but the biblical literature presents us with the most complex set of problems, because no other ancient book has been preserved in so many copies and, consequently, with so many variants. Of all the disciplines involved in the study of the New Testament it is in some ways the least far advanced. Many of the later manuscripts have never been studied in detail, and we are very far from a complete tabulation of the similarities and differences between all the manuscripts at our disposal, a task which would be impossible without a computer. Nevertheless much progress has been made, especially over the last century, and we now know a great deal more than the translators of the Authorized Version could know about the text of the New Testament.

In order to establish the original text, the first step is to understand the evidence with which we have to deal. It is of three main types: Greek manuscripts, versions in other languages, and quotations in early church writers. Of these the Greek manuscripts are the most important. They are usually subdivided into four main categories: papyri, uncials, minuscules and lectionaries.

Papyrus was the normal writing material of the Roman Empire. The pith of the papyrus reed was cut into strips and pressed together to form sheets. Ordinary books were made by joining the required number of sheets edge to edge to form a continuous length which could be rolled up. The text was written in columns on one side and, in rare cases, on the reverse. The earliest Christian scriptures we possess, however, are of a form which appears not to have come into more general use until much later. The sheets were folded and stitched in quires to form a *codex* or book. The text was then written on both sides. It is not known precisely when or why Christians, unlike their Jewish and Greek neighbours, adopted this method.

Only in the dry climate of Egypt have papyrus documents of any kind survived in quantity. Consequently we have only about eighty-five papyrus manuscripts of the New Testament. Most of these are no more than tiny fragments, a few verses, or a part of

17

a single book, but there are seven of greater length, covering between them most of the New Testament and named (after the two collectors who acquired them) the Chester Beatty and Bodmer papyri. The important feature of the papyrus manuscripts is their date. The earliest, a tiny fragment $2\frac{1}{2}$ inches by $3\frac{1}{2}$ inches of John chapter 18, has been dated around AD 125, and most of the others are to be dated in the second to fourth centuries. They are the oldest copies of the New Testament we possess.

Some time in the fourth century, probably about the time when the Emperor Constantine gave official recognition to Christianity and the church's prosperity began to increase, *vellum* or parchment was adopted by the church as a writing material instead of papyrus. A form of specially treated animal skin, it was thought in ancient times (probably mistakenly) to be more durable than papyrus and therefore very suitable for scriptures which needed to be carefully preserved. Apart from the papyri already mentioned, all our New Testament manuscripts are of this material.

Until about the ninth century the form of writing used in producing books (whether on papyrus or vellum) was a form of capital letters, known as *uncials*. While it had the advantage of clarity, the form was necessarily laborious, and in the ninth century a form of longhand was developed which enabled books to be copied more quickly without too great a sacrifice in legibility. This script was known as *minuscule* and eventually replaced the uncial script altogether, continuing in use up to and beyond the invention of printing. It is convenient to divide our vellum manuscripts into two categories according to the script used, the uncials being the earlier and smaller group.

Of these uncial manuscripts however only a few can be called really early. The earliest of all are those known as Codex Vaticanus and Codex Sinaiticus, the one named on account of its location in the Vatican library in Rome, the other because, so the story goes, it was discovered (by the German scholar Tischendorf in 1844) being used page by page to light the furnace of the monastery of St. Catherine on Mt. Sinai! These two manuscripts are to be dated in the fourth century. A few others may be almost as early, but most are later, the majority dating from the eighth and ninth centuries.

Papyri and uncials together account for only a tiny portion (about one-fifteenth) of the Greek manuscripts at our disposal. The rest are either minuscules of the ninth century and later or, a fourth category, *lectionaries*. These, in number about two thousand, are distinguished from other New Testament manuscripts not by the materials used or the style of writing, but by the fact that the text is presented in the form of selections for reading in worship, much as the epistle and gospel of the day are set out for every Sunday and feast day in the Book of Common Prayer. Both uncial and minuscule lectionaries exist, but few have been closely studied. Most of them apparently date from the eighth century or later.

The age of a manuscript is determined by a variety of tests. The history of the development of writing (palaeography) is a science in its own right, and documents can generally be dated to within fifty years by the formation of the letters alone. Radiological tests can also establish, within limits, the age of the material on which the text is written. In addition many manuscripts contain notes about the date and place at which they were written, the exemplar from which they were copied, and the name of the scribe. While there is some margin for disagreement among experts, particularly with early documents, the overall picture of the age of our manuscripts is not in doubt and its significance should not be missed. Of all the copies of the New Testament in the original Greek surviving from the fourteen-and-a-half centuries before the invention of printing, the vast majority date from the second half of the period, when most of the important variant readings current in the earlier stage had been forgotten or suppressed. It is about these earlier variants that we most need to know, but the evidence of the Greek manuscripts is sparse. We need to supplement it by information from other sources, the versions and the ancient Christian writers.

As early as the second century the books of the New Testament were translated, as the mission of the church came to require it. In particular they were translated into Latin in the west, Syriac in the East, later into Coptic in Egypt, and into other languages. These translations or *versions* are also preserved in manuscript form, so that we have problems in reconstructing the original text of each version which are similar to those facing

19

us in the case of the original Greek. The importance of the versions is twofold: first they were made from the Greek at a time earlier than the date of most of our surviving Greek manuscripts and are therefore important evidence for the wording of the underlying Greek text at that period; secondly we are fortunate in having some very early manuscripts of them.

In a similar way the quotations from the New Testament in the writings of *the early Fathers* are important evidence for the text of the New Testament at the date at which the quotations were made. The theological writers and preachers of the first five centuries quoted the Bible in debate and teaching, and composed commentaries upon the scriptures, thus giving indirect evidence of the biblical text of their day which, with the shortage of manuscripts surviving from the period, is very valuable. In the case of their writings too we have to face problems of textual criticism, and we cannot always be sure that they are quoting from a written text rather than from memory; but in spite of this it is often possible to establish the form of text used by an early Christian writer, and where this corresponds closely to the text contained in a New Testament manuscript or group of manuscripts in our possession, we can deduce that those manuscripts preserve the form of text in use in the church of the ancient writer's home area. In this way we are able to chart the areas in which various types of text circulated in the early centuries.

How are we to use this evidence to arrive at the original wording? It would be a mistake to assume that all we had to do in a given passage was to adopt the reading contained in the greatest number of manuscripts and other witnesses. It is not the number of witnesses but their value which counts. To take a hypothetical example: if we possess ten copies of a document now lost, two of which are copies of the original, differing from each other, and the remaining eight more or less exact copies of one of the first two, it would be an error to assume that the readings contained in the nine are more likely to be correct through weight of numbers than the readings in the odd one. Because the nine copies are all related to each other, we have only two witnesses, not ten, to what the original document read. For this reason it is vital to try to discover how manuscripts are related to each other, to group them according to their similarities and differences, and in this way to determine 'families' of manuscripts or types of text.

The age of a manuscript is also important. A variant reading in a late manuscript may have been introduced only at a very late stage in the process of copying. It does not follow from this that all variant readings occurring only in late manuscripts are to be rejected, for a late manuscript may have been copied from a very much earlier one, now lost, which also contained the variant. It does follow, however, that if the manuscript is early, the readings in it deserve to be treated seriously. This is why the papyri, the uncials and the evidence from the early Christian writers and early translations are more important than all the minuscules together.

Equally important for establishing the original wording of a given passage is a knowledge of the processes by which the wording may have been altered in copying books by hand. Many variant readings, as we have already suggested, would arise accidentally – a word misread, or a word or even a whole line omitted or repeated. Who has not heard an inexperienced reader make similar mistakes when reading the lessons in church? The possibility of such mistakes was of course recognized in ancient times, and efforts were usually made to check a manuscript after copying. Even so, errors slipped through. On occasions a later copyist, using the faulty manuscript as an exemplar for a further copy, would detect the fault and correct it. This however was a mixed blessing, for it is now apparent that sometimes a copyist working on a text which he did not fully understand would assume an error where there was none, and 'correct' it to what he presumed it should have read. Because the result made good sense it might well escape later detection, and so become yet another variant for the modern critic to account for.

Thus, in addition to the accidental variants, we have deliberate alterations. To some extent they were corrections in style, grammar and vocabulary, to eliminate obscurities or to make the wording conform to the tastes of a later age. But other motives could operate. In the gospels there was a tendency, probably largely unconscious, to make parallel versions of the same passage in Matthew, Mark and Luke conform to each other. An example of this is the way in which some manuscripts of

21

Luke, as we have seen, contain the Lord's Prayer in a form closer to that in Matthew. A further tendency in the gospels, particularly in the very early stages, was to make the written version of a saying or story of Jesus conform to some better known version in circulation by word of mouth at the time. The variant in the Lord's Prayer, *thy Holy Spirit come upon us and cleanse us* for *thy kingdom come*, is probably to be explained in this way. In some churches the tradition probably arose of saying the prayer in this 'improved' form because it made the meaning more intelligible to the congregation, and a scribe used to this version substituted it, perhaps even unconsciously, when copying out the gospel of Luke. There are many examples of items added to the text from oral tradition; for example, some manuscripts contain an additional saying after Luke 6: 4 – 'On the same day he saw someone working on the sabbath and said to him, "Man, if you know what you are doing, you are blessed; but if not, you are accursed, and a transgressor of the law."' A longer example is the story of the woman taken in adultery, which occurs at various places in different manuscripts, including John 7: 53, but is missing from the earliest copies of the gospels altogether.

Other alterations had a more deliberate doctrinal intention. They were attempts to make the New Testament conform to what later ages regarded as orthodoxy. It is clear that the ease with which dissident groups in the early church were able to quote biblical texts in support of their views was an embarrassment to their opponents, and steps were taken to amend some texts in a 'safer' direction. An example of this is probably to be found in Luke 2: 41, where in place of the phrase *his parents* some Latin manuscripts read *Joseph and Mary his mother,* thereby leaving no ambiguity about the virgin birth of Jesus.

By about AD 300 there was considerable variety in the texts of the New Testament in use in the church. As we have seen, it is often possible by classifying similarities of readings to establish the text of the New Testament in use in different geographical areas. That in use in the west (that is, in Italy, France and North Africa) differed at many points from those used in Northern Egypt but, for reasons not entirely clear to us, bore close resemblance to some texts used in Syria. In Egypt two types of text appear to have been in use, one of which probably owes much to the careful editorial attention of Christian scholars in Alexandria, where there was a long tradition of literary scholarship outside the church. The other was also in use at Caesarea. There were probably other types in other areas, less easily detected at this distance of time. Of all these the western text appears to have suffered most from additions and alterations.

Gradually, however, particularly after persecution ceased and Christians had more leisure for scholarly pursuits, attempts were made to produce a standardized text. Copies were compared and corrected and errors removed (although not necessarily by the application of what we should regard today as sound principles, as described below). This happened in connexion with a number of languages. The Vulgate Latin text, which still carries authority in the Roman Catholic Church, was the product of one attempt at revision. So far as the Greek was concerned, the text preferred by the church in Constantinople (the *Byzantine* or *Koine* text) eventually became the norm to which others were made to conform. Unfortunately it is not a generally reliable text. Those who produced it too often tried to compromise between alternative readings by including both, or by adopting the one most congenial to them. It needs to be judged critically like the other, earlier types of text. Almost all our late minuscules contain it, however, and the first printed Greek Bibles reproduced it. In time it formed the basis for the Authorized Version and other early English translations. Hence the need for new translations, based on a more reliable text.

There is thus no simple method of arriving at the original text of the New Testament. We do not possess the original copy of any part of it. Our earliest copies of any importance are between seventy-five and one hundred years later than the date at which the books they contain were probably written, and already contain many of the variant readings which persist at later times. Textual critics can do much to elucidate the history of the text; they can eliminate many variants as later emendations, and reduce the number of alternatives to be considered to the few which are known to have existed in the earliest period; but there is no infallible procedure to carry us back behind those alternatives to the original text. In the last resort a reasoned choice has to be made.

In making such choices, the textual critic will be guided by a number of considerations. What is the relative strength of the evidence for each of the alternatives? Are any manuscripts particularly unreliable because the scribes concerned were demonstrably prone to careless mistakes? How early is the evidence? Was one alternative widely known while another might be accounted for as a purely local variant? Is there any obvious reason, such as an error of spelling or copying, or a doctrinal correction, which would account for an alternative? Can any variant be explained as an attempt to harmonize two others, or to smooth over a difficulty? The general rule which the critic follows is that, in choosing the reading which he regards as original, he must also show how, given that reading, the alternatives before him might naturally have arisen as errors or corrections. Because the tendency among scribes was to expand the text to ensure nothing was lost, the modern scholar will normally prefer the shorter reading. Similarly because scribes tended to eliminate difficulties he will prefer the more difficult reading. But these are no more than rules of thumb. The critic's decision will depend in every case on the balance of probability when all the relevant factors have been considered. In the majority of instances the verdict of scholars is unanimous, but it can never, in the nature of the case, reach the level of absolute proof. There is always the possibility that with the discovery of yet more manuscripts, or further research into those already available, new evidence may come to light to cast doubt on assured conclusions.

In the light of this it is natural to ask how far textual criticism can affect the message of the New Testament. If it has no effect at all one may feel that it is hardly worth bothering about; if on the other hand the meaning of the New Testament can be changed by adopting alternative readings at strategic places, important questions need to be asked about the basis upon which the critic prefers one set of readings to another, and the objectivity of his judgement. There have certainly been occasions in the past when textual scholars have been vigorously attacked for 'undermining Scripture' because they omitted verses which in their judgement were late interpolations, but which to their critics were indispensable foundations of orthodox doctrine. When, in the sixteenth century, the biblical scholar Erasmus published a printed edition of the Greek New Testament omitting I John 5: 7, 'For there are three witnesses in heaven, the Father, the Word and the Holy Spirit, and these three are one,' the Christian world was outraged, and he was later persuaded to reintroduce it. Today its absence from the New English Bible is not even marked by a footnote!

It is important to stress, however, that the 'message of the New Testament' cannot rest on isolated verses. If the phrase means anything at all, it must denote those convictions and affirmations which are shared by all, or at least a majority of New Testament writers. It is to be deduced from the totality of what they say, rather than from individual sentences taken separately. Revising the text of individual sentences in the light of variant manuscript readings will not therefore make any important difference to the kind of generalization which is necessary for so broad a concept as 'the message of the New Testament'. Adopting alternative readings will certainly affect the precise interpretation of particular passages and consequently our understanding of the detailed thought of a writer. An important case in point is Luke 23: 34, where some of the best known words from the cross, 'Father, forgive them, for they do not know what they are doing,' although probably original are missing from quite a wide range of early witnesses. Our judgement of this will obviously affect our understanding of the crucifixion of Jesus, although only one gospel is involved.

Many variant readings, on the other hand, are of a quite trivial nature and there is no question of our understanding of Christianity as such being threatened or radically altered by any of them. Indeed on the whole textual criticism strengthens our confidence in the New Testament. By comparison with all other ancient books which have survived from antiquity, our knowledge of the New Testament is truly vast. In the case of many other books the text is often so corrupt, and the evidence on which to recover it so scanty, that the editor has to resort to conjecture in many places. For the New Testament we have such a wealth of evidence that conjecture (in the opinion of most scholars) is hardly ever to be contemplated, if at all. The presence of the many variant readings with which textual criticism deals must be kept in perspective. The fact that for so much of the New Testament so many witnesses agree about the wording is a testimony to the general faithfulness with which it has been handed down to us.

There are two important aspects, however, in which the study of textual criticism does affect our approach to the New Testament and our estimate of what it is. In the first place, as we have already seen, many of the most striking variant readings arose in the very earliest period, up to AD 200. They cannot be explained simply on the basis that, with poor communications between churches in one part of the world and another and with the pressures of persecution, it was impossible to keep a check on errors which crept into the texts in use in various localities. Alternative texts were in use *in the same place*. Origen, the scholar and theologian of Alexandria, and later of Caesarea (c. 185–254), is known to have used two or three different versions. In certain cases too, as we have seen, changes were deliberately made. Christians of the earliest period took liberties with the text of the New Testament which we would not feel free to take today, and which their Jewish neighbours did not feel free to take with the Old. The state of the text is a reflection of the fact that the New Testament writings only gradually acquired the status of Holy Scripture, and while Christians were generally more conservative with the text of their literature than their non-Jewish neighbours with the Greek and Latin classics, the sense of what was written mattered more to them than the precise wording.

The other consideration points in the same direction. Not only in the state of the text but in the works they contain the manuscripts of the New Testament are evidence for the slow way in which the New Testament grew. One papyrus of the third century contains Jude and the two letters of Peter amidst a whole series of apocryphal writings, spurious letters of Paul, psalms and hymns and other early Christian documents. Even the great Codex Sinaiticus, written perhaps a hundred years later, contains along with the Old and New Testaments as we know them and without any discrimination from them, two second-century writings, the Epistle of Barnabas and the Shepherd of Hermas. The New Testament, as a restricted collection of books, was still in process of formation. But this leads us on to a consideration of the New Testament Canon.

3. How It Came Together

Although we often refer to 'the Bible' as though it were a single book, we need to remind ourselves that there is no universal agreement about its contents. While all Protestants agree on an Old Testament of thirty-nine books and a New of twenty-seven, they differ on the status, if any, to be accorded to the collection of fifteen books and parts of books known as the Old Testament Apocrypha. Most copies of the Bible used by Protestants omit them or include them as a separate section. The Roman Catholic Church, on the other hand, regards twelve of these books as an equal part of the Bible, and includes them dispersed among the rest of the Old Testament. The Eastern Orthodox Churches accept only four of them – Tobit, Judith, Ecclesiasticus and Wisdom – rejecting the rest. Nor is the Old Testament alone affected. The Church in Ethiopia, for many centuries cut off for various historical and geographical reasons from the rest of Christendom, still retains a Bible containing additional books in both Old and New Testaments.

The reason for these differences is that in origin the Bible was not a single volume, but a collection of books which were first produced separately, at various times over a long period, and gradually brought into association with each other, the Old Testament first and later, by addition, the books of the New. We need not consider here the formation of the Old Testament, but we must try to trace some of the developments which led to the gospels, Acts, epistles and Revelation being regarded as belonging together and having authority for the church.

The word 'Canon', with reference to the New Testament, means an officially defined list of books accepted by the church as its sacred scriptures. The word did not come into use until about the fourth century, but the idea was present long before. Certainly by the middle of the second century the need to draw up such a list was making itself felt. It is not easy to trace the

27

development in detail, however, because of lack of evidence, particularly for the earlier periods.

The evidence available to us is of three kinds. The first comprises formal lists and discussions, in Christian writers and the records of synods, of the books to be accepted as authoritative. These are the most helpful, because the authors intended them to be comprehensive. In some cases lists of rejected books are also given. Most of this evidence, however, dates from the third century and later.

A second type of evidence is provided, as we have already seen in the last chapter, by the contents of New Testament manuscripts. This must be treated with caution, for we cannot assume that a manuscript was intended to include all accepted writings, but the inclusion of additional books which we no longer regard as scriptural may in some cases show that the books included were regarded as being on an equal footing.

The third type of evidence is derived from an analysis of early Christian writings. We can list the books which the writers quote, or of which they betray knowledge by echoing language and ideas without explicit quotation, and we may be able to deduce from their references the kind of esteem in which they held them. This line of enquiry also has its difficulties because we cannot necessarily assume from the fact that an author did not quote a book that he did not know it, or that he did not accept it as authoritative. Arguments from silence of this kind only have weight when corroborated by our other types of evidence. For example, it is probably accidental that Polycarp, Bishop of Smyrna, writing about AD 125, appears not to refer to I Thessalonians. He certainly knows II Thessalonians and a number of Paul's other letters. On the other hand the fact that no writer of the early second century shows any knowledge of II Peter is significant when it is also noted that it is absent from a list of authoritative books produced about AD 200 and when writers of the third century refer to it as 'disputed'. In spite of these ambiguities, this third type of evidence is all we have for the crucial first half of the second century.

As with the study of the text of the New Testament, so too with the history of the Canon, we have to remember that there was no uniformity in the ancient church. Travel was difficult, particularly for the social classes which made up the majority of church members, and in consequence developments in some areas were not matched elsewhere. We cannot assume that the evidence for one locality held good for that period throughout the world. Sometimes we have direct evidence of contemporary writers disagreeing. The outstanding cases are Hebrews and Revelation. For a long time hesitations were expressed in the western churches about accepting Hebrews as a letter of Paul even when its intrinsic value was acknowledged, while Revelation was accepted without question. In the eastern churches the reverse was usually the case: Hebrews was included, Revelation was not.

It is not the purpose of this book to offer a detailed history of the development of the Canon. It is inevitably complex and can be fully understood only against the background of the history of the church in the period. Even in the general survey which follows we shall have to take for granted some of the results of the detailed study of the New Testament which we shall describe in later chapters. Four main phases can be distinguished, although one should not think of them as sharply defined periods, for they overlap each other.

(1) The first phase can be roughly called the apostolic – that is, the period when the apostles were alive and the earlier books of the New Testament were being composed (roughly up to AD 70). At this early stage the Canon of the Old Testament itself was not yet finally closed; of the three sections into which the Jewish Scriptures were divided, the contents of the Law (Genesis to Deuteronomy) and the Prophets (Joshua, Judges, Samuel, Kings, Isaiah, Jeremiah, Ezekiel, and Hosea to Malachi) were fixed, but there was still uncertainty about some of the remaining books. These however were the Scriptures of the earliest church. From the very first, Christians regarded them as their own and not merely borrowed from Judaism. At the beginning they possessed no other sacred books at all, and although in the course of time they began to produce their own literature, of which the letters of Paul are the earliest to survive, they did not at this stage regard them in the same category as Holy Scripture. On the contrary the only authority which the Christians acknowledged alongside the Old Testament was not a book but a living voice, that of the Lord Jesus. He was both alongside the Scriptures and over them; alongside, for he did not replace them, yet

at the same time over them, for they pointed to him and he revealed their true meaning. His voice was to be heard in several ways, in the tradition of his words and deeds passed on by word of mouth, in the teaching of the apostles who were invested with his authority, and in the prophetic word spoken by Christian prophets under the influence of the Spirit. However, such prophetic pronouncements were not an infallible guide to the Lord's will; the church quickly learned that prophets had to be tested. Often too the apostles were not available, and most congregations must from the very beginning have relied upon traditions of apostolic teaching left with them by an apostle on his founding visit or passed on to them by whoever had first brought them the gospel. As time went on, therefore, it was natural that they should turn for guidance to letters the apostles had written, and that at the end of the period the first attempts should be made to set down in writing the words and deeds of Jesus. The all-important point however is that for this phase the authority of the Lord Jesus was not essentially embodied in a written tradition. Written documents were secondary to the living voice. The only written authority was the Old Testament, now considered as Christian Scripture.

(2) The second phase lasted from the end of the apostolic age to about AD 150. Our information about it is scanty and a number of questions remain at present unanswered. One of these concerns the process by which writings originally composed for a single church, or for churches in a particular area, became known elsewhere. How, for example, were Paul's letters assembled? Did the collection grow gradually, in snowball fashion, as Christians began to share the letters with each other (cf. Colossians 4: 16), or was there (as some scholars have suggested) a deliberate decision by some unknown person to search for them, edit and publish them, in order to prevent their being irretrievably lost? Again, how did we come to have our four gospels? Unless Luke 1:1 is an exaggeration, gospels were written in the early period which never attained to general circulation and were lost for ever. How did these four rise to pre-eminence, in spite of the fact that three of them overlap considerably? In this connexion we are at a disadvantage because it is not always easy to discover what gospels were being used by early second-century writers. Exact quotations from our

30

gospels are rare; when sayings of Jesus are quoted it is often not certain whether they represent inexact quotations from our gospels, quotations from other gospels now lost, or unwritten sayings which were known to the writer through oral tradition. We know that even a hundred years after the crucifixion, oral traditions about Jesus were felt by some to be more reliable than written records.

In spite of these uncertainties, some features of this second phase of development are clear. It is generally agreed that during this period the later portions of the New Testament were written. So too were other letters and pamphlets called forth by the need of the times, such as the correspondence of Ignatius, Bishop of Antioch, with the churches he visited on his journey to martyrdom in Rome about the year 107, or Clement's letter from Rome to Corinth, written about 96. In addition a large variety of works, some still surviving in fragmentary form, others known only by name, were produced in imitation of those now in the New Testament: gospels, acts and apocalypses attributed to various apostles and other groups. Some of these latter were designed to advocate a particular point of view; others were mere romances, and can have had only limited vogue. 'Scripture' however continued to mean the Old Testament, and much time was devoted to giving it a Christian interpretation. The general authorities for the life of the church were still the Old Testament on the one hand and the teaching of Jesus on the other, but there was now a growing recognition that the church was living after the age of the apostles and looking back to them; the need to rely on written records was making itself felt. The custom developed of reading Christian writings alongside the Old Testament in worship. This was a natural development because some, perhaps most, had originally been intended to be read in a gathering of the church for which they were produced, presumably in worship (Colossians 4:16, Revelation 1:3). Although none, as far as we can detect, was produced with the intention of its ranking as sacred scripture, they came by stages which we cannot now trace to be read on a regular basis and in a larger number of churches. By the end of the period the four gospels and Acts, Paul's letters, Hebrews, some of the other letters, and Revelation were widely known and quoted, but they were far from unique in this respect. Other Christian works were used alongside them. They were gaining in authority, but no one, it seems, had yet thought of defining what that authority was, how it was related to the Old Testament, or precisely which books possessed it.

(3) The third phase, lasting approximately from AD 150 to 200, marks the emergence of the New Testament as a defined collection with the status of Scripture. It is in this period that the term 'New Testament' is first used, by Irenaeus, Bishop of Lyons in about 180, to distinguish the writings of the New Covenant from the Scriptures of the Old. Their enhanced status was doubtless due largely to the custom of reading them alongside the Old Testament in worship. They now represented the authority of the Lord which the church had always recognized.

From the same period we have the earliest formal lists of Christian scriptures. By 200 the general lines of the contents of the New Testament were laid down, although there were still some variations. In the west generally, Hebrews was not included, or at least not regarded as being by Paul, while in the east the Revelation of John was suspect. II and III John, James and Jude were sometimes omitted, while II Peter is never even mentioned. Most of the other literature produced in phase two is by now firmly excluded, but a few works still find a place occasionally in the lists. Of the main part of the New Testament – gospels, Acts, letters of Paul – there is no longer any doubt.

The most important reason for this greater precision as to the contents of the New Testament was the need to define the church's position over against rival interpretations of its message. On the one hand there was the growing body of alternative literature which we have already mentioned. As the frequent use of the names of apostles in their titles implies, their authors felt themselves to be expressing legitimate elements in the Christian heritage derived from the apostles, and sought recognition for their work as such. In some cases the groups in which these works circulated distinguished themselves from the main body of Christians, and regarded their teaching as the only legitimate expression of Christian truth. In such cases it was not difficult for their opponents to respond by labelling them and their writings heretical. But in many cases the issues were not so clear, and the task which Christian writers and leaders undertook of determining which books could legitimately be used in the church, both in public teaching and in private study, was part of the general process of defining Christianity.

In addition to this problem, which was met by a process of exclusion, there was also a threat from the other direction. Marcion, a native of Asia Minor who later moved to Rome, developed in about the year 140 the view that the God of the Old Testament was a lesser being from whom Christians were delivered by the God of Jesus, and accordingly put out his own form of scriptures. These completely excluded the Old Testament, and there remained only ten letters of Paul (not those to Timothy and Titus) and the gospel of Luke, all rigorously edited. Reaction to his teaching undoubtedly led to the church's asserting in a more positive way than hitherto the value of the Scriptures which it did accept.

(4) The final phase can be dealt with more briefly. It lasted from about AD 200 into the fifth century. The New Testament in use was substantially that which we now have, but differences of opinion continued on the one hand over Hebrews, Revelation, James, Jude, II Peter, II and III John, all of which gradually won their way to full acceptance, and on the other hand over the Shepherd of Hermas, the (so-called) Letter of Barnabas, I Clement and similar works, which were eventually rejected. By the middle of the fifth century by far the majority of Christians were using all the books which we use now. There were still remote places which retained a more conservative view. In areas of the church in Syria as late as the fourteenth century only one Letter of Peter and one of John were recognized, and Jude and Revelation not at all. But this was a church no longer in communion with the main part of Christendom because of doctrinal differences. As we have seen, for similar reasons the church in Ethiopia also retained a distinctive canon. But for the main part of the church the Canon, so far as the New Testament was concerned, was settled by about 450. The earliest list which contains exactly those books which we now recognize is in a letter of Athanasius of 367.

What were the guiding principles behind this process of inclusion? For process it was; no single decision was ever taken by a central authority to fix for the whole church the contents of the New Testament. Council decisions, where they were taken, merely recorded what was already the case. In theory, the test which was applied for inclusion in the Canon, particularly in the later stages, was apostolic authorship. But such a test was never rigidly applied. It was always acknowledged that two of the gospels were not written by apostles, but they were defended on the grounds that their authors were associates of apostles – Mark of Peter, Luke of Paul. If this seems like rationalization, it shows that these two Gospels were too well established to be struck off the list, no matter who had written them. On the other hand the claim to apostolic authority by itself could not guarantee a book's acceptance. There is an interesting story of Serapion, Bishop of Antioch about AD 190, who on a visit to the church in Rhossus was asked to give permission for the gospel of Peter to be read in church. Not being aware at the time of its contents he agreed, but on returning home he made a study of it and concluded that it denied the reality of the humanity of Jesus. In consequence he wrote forbidding its further use, and promising to visit the church again to put their doctrine right! The real criterion, in other words, was apostolicity of content rather than authorship. Books were judged on whether their teaching agreed with the church's understanding of the gospel as handed down from apostolic times. In practice this meant an appeal to the consensus of Christian judgement in the churches. One reason why later ages rejected books which had earlier been accepted was that the nature of Christianity became more clearly defined. Lines of development from the faith and practice of the church in the New Testament period, which were open options in the second century, were rejected in the third and fourth by the main body of Christians because it was seen more clearly where they would lead.

To some extent the process had to be circular: the church's understanding of the faith was formed by the New Testament books, read in worship and used as a basis for teaching; the decision as to which books were acceptable for teaching and worship was based on the church's understanding of the faith. But there were safeguards against complete circularity. In no period has the faith of the church been nurtured only by its scriptures, but also by worship, preaching, personal example, and all those other elements of faith and life which go under the general heading of 'tradition'. Furthermore writers like Eusebius, Bishop of Caesarea in the mid-fourth century, in listing the books to be approved and rejected, appealed not merely to local custom, but to the practice of the wider church, including Christian writers of earlier periods, even though the result was that in respect of some books he had to record that there was no agreement. Thus, while there has never been one, definitive, universally binding decision for the whole church on the Canon, nevertheless it can be said that the New Testament is the product of the common judgement of the church over several centuries.

This is not to say, as is often claimed, that 'the church created the Canon'. It was essentially a growing recognition that certain books alone held authority for the church and, more important, that others did not, but contained teaching which was repugnant. The idea of authority is in fact the crucial issue. The motive was to preserve for the church the authority of the Lord and his apostles by which from the beginning its life had been regulated, and which these particular writings were felt to express.

It is important to bear this in mind when considering whether the limits of the Canon are still valid in the light of modern biblical criticism. From time to time the question is raised whether we should continue with the traditional Canon or attempt to revise it. As we shall see, the real authorship of most parts of the New Testament is disputed by many scholars, and the date of composition is often put late in the first century or even, in some cases, well into the second. If we were to take apostolic authorship as the qualification for inclusion in the New Testament, it is doubtful whether more than a few letters of Paul would remain. If, on the other hand, we chose a date as the criterion, we should either have to fix it so early as to exclude some much-loved writings, including at least one Gospel, or so late as to include works not at present in the New Testament, such as Clement of Rome's first letter which is probably contemporary with Revelation. But, as we have seen, neither date nor authorship was the original criterion, and we are not dealing with the simple task of correcting ancient mistakes, but with the fundamental issue of authority. By what shall the church define its faith? What shall provide its categories of thought, the mental images which inspire its worship, the starting-point for its decisions about right and wrong, the key by which to understand itself?

Viewed in this light, the New Testament is evidence not only of what the church believed in the period in which it was written, but of what the church believed, and felt itself bound by, in the period in which the Canon was formed. It was one of the ways by which the growing church defined itself; and wherever she has continued to accept that Canon, she has continued to define herself – at least partly – in those terms, and declared her continuity with the church of the past. In this sense the Canon can never be revised. It is a fact of history: we can no more change what the early church felt impelled to include in it, than we can alter what St. Augustine wrote in his *Confessions*, or Pope John XXIII in his *Diary of a Soul*. We either accept it as it stands, as part of our identifying ourselves with the ancient Christians from whom we have received it, or we reject it and their understanding of Christian faith along with it, substituting an alternative of our own.

There are those who would prefer to do the latter. Modern study of the New Testament has tended to emphasize the diversity of viewpoints, even contradictions, contained in it, and it has been argued that in the light of this we must define more precisely which viewpoints are authoritative and which are not. Thus we must treat the sayings of Jesus or the undisputed letters of Paul as the definitive points of the New Testament, the 'canon within the Canon'. In practice we all do this. Just as very few of those who affirm the creeds give equal emphasis to every clause, or believe precisely and only what their composers meant by them, in the same way few of those who are happy to accept the traditional Canon in practice regulate their faith and conduct by everything contained in all the books. It might then seem more honest to limit the Canon to those parts which we do accept in practice. In fact such an ideal would be unattainable, for both churches and individuals differ on the emphasis which they give to different parts of the Canon. Each person would end up with his own particular Bible, a collection of favourite passages which might even vary for the same individual at different times. The point of the Canon is not that it records precisely what we now believe, whether as individuals or collectively, but that it attests what the church has believed in the past. In origin the word 'canon' means a measuring-rod or rule, and this well describes the New Testament. It is not descriptive but regulative. It does not describe Christian faith exhaustively, but sets limits to what may properly be called Christian. It acts as a norm or standard by which to measure ourselves. In its selection of contents, as well as in its text, language and ideas, the New Testament is an ancient book and cannot be modernized. It can only be interpreted and used.

4. Analysing the Documents

An important aspect of the study of the New Testament is concerned with what is generally known as 'introduction'. In part this covers questions of text and canon which we have already considered; in part it is concerned with the date, genuineness, authorship and composition of the documents, and the historical circumstances in which they were written. Its importance lies not simply in the general interest of such questions but in the fact that it is an indispensable preparation for interpreting what the documents say. We saw in connexion with the Lord's Prayer that the question which version Jesus actually taught cannot be answered, unless we first discover the relationship between the Gospels of Matthew and Luke, in which the two principal versions of the prayer are preserved. Similarly we cannot fully understand the meaning of any writer without discovering who he was, to whom he was writing and why, and the general background against which he and his readers were living. In practice the answer to these questions may have to be sought chiefly or even exclusively in what he has written; but the converse is still true, that we shall not fully understand what he has written until all the available facts have been brought out and allowed to shed light upon the text.

In view of the importance of these questions we shall begin this chapter by illustrating the methods employed, before looking at some of the questions which are often raised by it. We start with a straightforward and relatively uncontroversial example.

In chapter three we saw that, while the gospels and the letters of Paul became acknowledged relatively quickly as indisputable parts of the New Testament, some other books were questioned for much longer, and only gradually won their way to universal acceptance. Particularly was this true of the second letter of Peter. There is no certain reference to this work, nor any quotation from it, in Christian writers until the early third century, and even two hundred years later the majority rejected it. Although it was eventually accepted by the main churches in both east and west, it was a latecomer to the lists, and for many centuries maintained its position only with difficulty. Of all the books in the New Testament the status of II Peter is the most precarious.

At first sight this seems strange. It opens unambiguously 'From Simeon [i.e. Simon] Peter, servant and apostle of Jesus Christ . . .' (II Peter 1:1). In the first chapter there is an explicit reference to the transfiguration of Jesus on the mountain, and to the author's presence there (1:16-18). The third chapter opens with a reference back to a previous letter, and various details confirm that the author is referring to I Peter (3:1). Later in this chapter there is a reference to the letters of 'our beloved brother Paul'. II Peter clearly purports to be a letter written by the apostle Peter, and the hesitation felt about it by the early church is therefore surprising. Nevertheless scholars today almost unanimously uphold these early doubts, and concede that it is not genuine. Their reasons for doing so can be considered under six headings.

(1) The first reason is the situation with which the letter deals. II Peter is designed to warn its readers against the threat posed to the church by the teaching of certain unnamed people, whom the writer plainly considers to be heretical. His case against them is based partly on their behaviour, for they boast of a 'freedom' which he sees to be immoral and even bestial, partly on their irreverent attitude to what is sacred, but chiefly on their contempt for the Christian expectation of the return of Christ. All this has put them outside the true Christian community to which they once belonged. In spite of this their teaching is apparently proving attractive to others, based as it is on 'private' interpretations of the Old Testament and the letters of Paul. The writer calls upon his readers to remain loyal to the truth which they have received from the Old Testament, from Christ himself, and from the apostles, and to keep themselves unstained by worldly lusts. If God is delaying the arrival of the last day, this is due to his mercy, to give men more time for repentance. The readers must remain steadfast, for the day of judgement will surely come, and then, if they have kept themselves pure, they will enter into Christ's kingdom as he has promised, and share the divine nature.

39

There are good grounds for thinking that this situation did not arise until well after Peter's death. Of course if we could identify the teachers with certainty, we should be able to determine the date at once, but we do not know enough to do so, and over-confident attempts to identify them with known second-century groups, or any others, have to be resisted. Nevertheless there are grounds for thinking that we are dealing with conflicts which arose later than the time of Peter. In the early days of the church the return of Jesus in glory and the end of the world were expected in the near future, certainly within the lifetime of most of the first converts (Romans 13:11f, I Corinthians 15:51f; cf. Mark 9:1, Matthew 16:28). Paul's first letter to the Thessalonians (4:13-18) shows that the death of some Christians before Jesus' expected return had caused some consternation in the church there. Evidently they had been led to anticipate that they would all still be alive when the end came. Now it would not be surprising if continued delay and the lengthening roll of the dead led to a questioning of this general expectation and to some shifts of emphasis in Christian teaching, and there is evidence in various parts of the New Testament that this is what happened. But the objection voiced by the 'false teachers' opposed by II Peter implies more than a shift of emphasis. The expectation is dismissed altogether as an illusion. 'Where now is the promise of his coming? Our fathers have been laid to their rest, but still everything continues exactly as it has always been since the world began' (3:4). The point has been passed where people can any longer acquiesce in talk of a 'delay': the radical question is now being asked whether it is right to speak of an 'end' to history at all. Have not things remained constant since the beginning of creation and will they not therefore continue unchanged for ever? The point to be grasped here is that questioning of this kind is not likely to arise while it is still credible to speak of waiting a little longer before the end. Only when the end has been postponed for so long that repetition of talk of its imminence becomes formal and unreal is it likely that the expectation will be denied altogether. We should not therefore expect such attitudes to arise in the early period, perhaps not at all within the lifetime of the first generation of Christians. This judgement is confirmed by the actual words attributed to the dissidents: the 'fathers', that is the first Christians who ought to have witnessed the

Lord's return, have all been 'laid to their rest'. These are the objections of the second generation, for whom the age of the apostles and the first converts is past. II Peter is dealing not with a problem contemporary with the apostle Peter but with one that arose later.

(2) This judgement is confirmed by the way the letter deals with the problem. It is cast in the form of a prediction of troubles to come. Peter is represented as reminding his readers of his teaching, just before his death, in order to guard them against false doctrine which will arise afterwards (1:12-14, 2:1). Much of this epistle is therefore written in the future tense. Of course, if the letter were really written by Peter, this would be just what we should expect, and prediction of future dangers must not be ruled out from the start as impossible; but the standpoint is not sustained. From 2:13 to the end of the chapter the writer suddenly begins to speak of the adversaries as contemporaries, using the present and even the past tense. In so doing he reveals his true concern. He is really writing about a *contemporary* problem and it is only the need to adopt the guise of an apostle, now dead, which has imposed on him the use of the future tense which he has not succeeded in carrying through.

A comparison with the letter of Jude is instructive here. This letter too deals with the problems caused by those who mock the traditional forms of Christian faith. One of the points the writer makes in reply is to remind his readers that there is no need for them to be surprised by such attacks, because the apostles had warned them repeatedly in the past to expect them (Jude v. 17). The writer of II Peter is making the same point, but by a different method. Instead of reminding his readers of apostolic teaching they had received in the past, he spells out the teaching for them in the guise of an apostle writing about the future.

(3) There is further support for this conclusion in the reference to Paul in 3:15f. II Peter is unique among New Testament writings in referring to 'all Paul's letters', implying a collection of them (although without any indication of its contents), and in regarding them as scripture of equal weight with the 'other scriptures'. (These 'other scriptures' consist apparently of the Old Testament and perhaps other writings also.) The attribution of scriptural standing to Paul's letters suggests a second-century date. We saw in the last chapter that the letters of Paul, like

41

other New Testament writings, only gradually attained the status of Scripture during that century. If such a view had in fact been held by the apostle Peter it is astonishing that it left no other mark upon the New Testament, or upon subsequent developments in the history of the Canon.

(4) Various aspects of the teaching of the epistle also give grounds for suspicion. The third chapter is devoted to a vindication of the hope of the Lord's coming which was being called in question. The writer denies the claim that everything continues exactly as it has always been since the world began by referring to a previous destruction at the time of the flood, and insists both that God's time-scale differs from ours (so that from the divine point of view there is no delay) and that in any case we should be grateful for the apparent delay as a sign of God's mercy in giving us longer time in which to repent. When the end comes it will be, like the flood, a time of punishment. Certain differences of emphasis, however, are noticeable in comparison with other New Testament writings, particularly I Peter. In the New Testament generally *last day* or *last days* (and similar expressions) means the period leading up to, and culminating in the end of the world and the beginning of the kingdom of God. Two different emphases are discernible. Sometimes from the point of view of the writer the last days are still in the future (James 5:3), or are just beginning, as contemporary events are held to indicate (I John 2:18). The dominant emphasis, however, is that the last days began with the coming of Jesus, and particularly with his resurrection and the coming of the Holy Spirit (Acts 2:17, Heb. 1:2, etc.). From this point of view the church from the beginning has always been living in the last days, although it may still look forward to their completion. In I Peter both of these emphases are to be found (cf. 1:5 with 1:3 and 20). In the second epistle, however, the second conviction is missing. *The last days* refers only to the coming day of judgement and to the emergence of false teachers as a sign of it. Nor does the writer in any other way express the conviction that the resurrection of Jesus has ushered in a new era. On the contrary, Old Testament prophets, Jesus and the apostles all appear together, without any radical differentiation between them, as belonging from the readers' point of view to a past age (cf. II Peter 1:12-21).

Also characteristic of II Peter is an emphasis on the future coming of Christ as a time of judgement, reward for the right-eous, punishment for the wicked, and the dissolution of the world by fire (2:9; 3:7-13). To be sure this theme is to be found elsewhere in the New Testament, but it is generally set against the background of a wider and more positive emphasis. Starting from the conviction that Christ was crucified by men, but was raised victorious from the dead by the Father and exalted to his right hand, most writers look forward to the coming of Christ as the time of his public glorification, when evil will be finally defeated, the world will be restored to its former glory and he will be acknowledged by all as Lord. These ideas are echoed by occasional phrases in II Peter, but the emphasis has shifted generally from the vindication of Christ to the judgement of men, and to the bare notion of the dissolution of the universe. In contrast to I Peter it is striking that the second letter has nothing to say about the resurrection of Jesus, and takes only his trans-figuration on the mountain as the proof of his coming glory (1:16-18).

Perhaps equally striking is the lack of references to the Holy Spirit. Of course not every book in the New Testament betrays the same interest in each aspect of doctrine, nor should it be expected to do so. Yet it is striking how many writings in the New Testament bear witness to the fact that the Holy Spirit was a dominant factor in the life and experience of the early church. II Peter is one of the few exceptions; the only reference to the Spirit, in 1:21, refers to the inspiration of the Old Testament prophets.

These points are aspects of what is often referred to as the 'early catholicism' of II Peter. During the second century the church developed certain characteristic institutions and doct-rines which have remained with her ever since. One of these was the three ministerial orders of bishops, presbyters and deacons, and the association of the bishop particularly with responsibility for preserving and teaching true doctrine. Another was the understanding of Christianity as involving a fixed body of teaching to be preserved and handed on, with the result that faith came to mean predominantly the giving of assent to such teaching, which could itself be called 'the faith'. Much stress was laid upon right behaviour, and Christianity came to be seen as a way of life in obedience to a new law promulgated by Christ.

Again, while the temporal dimension of Christianity was not lost, and the faithful continued to be directed to look forward to the impending day of judgement and to prepare for it by purity of life, the emphasis was laid no longer on a future transformation of this world but on an already existing heavenly realm, eternal and unchanging, which co-existed with this temporal and changing world, and to which the worshipper was introduced through the sacraments so that at death he might be received into it.

The seeds of these developments can of course be traced back to the earliest parts of the New Testament, but nevertheless they are substantially *developments* of what we find there. It is noticeable that in the New Testament, particularly in the letters of St. Paul, we have evidence of other emphases which tend to drop out of sight later. Church life and doctrine are less rigidly ordered and uniform. There is no clear evidence of a threefold order of ministry. Faith more often means an attitude of trust and commitment than assent to a body of doctrine. There is less emphasis on a legal code of behaviour and more stress on the freedom and responsibility of the Christian to discern for himself what is right under the guidance of the Spirit. In time the early exuberance, variety and openness of the church seems to have gradually settled down under various pressures, including persecution and the need to preserve the message from distortion, into something more regular and more prosaic. It is a matter of debate how early the transition began. Sometimes the assumption is made that it is a second-century development, and on these grounds alone any parts of the New Testament which bear strong traces of it are claimed to date from that period. This is too doctrinaire, for some stages may have been reached much earlier. The striking fact remains, however, that so many of the features of early catholicism are to be found all together in II Peter. In addition to those we have already observed we may note that the interpretation of the Scriptures is restricted, and not to be permitted to private individuals (1:20f); there are frequent references to the 'commandment', the 'truth' which has been handed on to the readers from the apostles and to which they must adhere (1:12, 2:21, 3:2); the readers are called on to escape the corruption of a transient world so that they may become 'partakers of the divine nature' by the practice of virtue

(1:4-8). Nowhere else in the New Testament are there such clear instances of ideas which later became commonplace nor so few instances of ideas which were certainly common in the earliest days. These characteristics are the more striking for being absent from I Peter. The authorship of the first epistle is also disputed, but we must at least admit that it is difficult to see how both letters could have emanated from the same mind.

(5) For most scholars the feature of II Peter which clinches the question of its authenticity is its relation to the letter of Jude. As any reader can see who cares to make the comparison, virtually the whole of the contents of Jude are incorporated into II Peter, chiefly in the second chapter. While it is not a word-for-word copy, II Peter includes the basic ideas of Jude, and much of the actual language. Like II Peter, Jude is written to attack teaching which was undermining the moral standards of the church, although Jude knows nothing of attacks on the expectation of the Lord's return. It is easier to envisage the writer of II Peter taking over Jude and adding extra material to fit a new situation, than to imagine Jude being based on II Peter, but omitting nearly two-thirds of it. Further, some of the references in Jude are more clear and precise than the parallels in II Peter (cf. Jude v. 9 with II Peter 2:11), and are best explained as the originals to which II Peter more vaguely alludes. It is therefore generally agreed that Jude is the earlier of the two works.

The identity of the author of Jude is not certain. The way he introduces himself as 'Jude, a servant of Jesus Christ and brother of James' suggests that we are to think of one of the brothers of Jesus (Mark 6:3). Opinions differ as to whether this Jude could have written the epistle; a decision is difficult because we know very little about him. What is indisputable is that at the time of writing the author of Jude looks back on the age of the apostles as a bygone age (verses 17f). This clearly rules out the possibility that Peter could still have been alive to incorporate Jude's letter into his own, unless by some chance Peter had outlived all his contemporaries. There is no hint in Christian tradition that he did.

(6) The final confirmation of our doubts comes from the hesitations from which we began that were long felt in the early church about accepting II Peter. What the foundation of these hesitations was we do not know. Perhaps they were based only

on the dim memory that it did not come into circulation until long after it should have appeared if it had been genuine, but they fully confirm the results of modern study. It is unthinkable that a letter of Peter, known to be genuine, should have been so widely ignored. There seems to be no alternative therefore to the conclusion that the letter was not written by the apostle Peter but by someone else using his name, and should probably be dated in the second century. Many scholars date it near 150.

We have considered II Peter in some detail because there is very little controversy about the judgements we have advanced, and it thus serves to illustrate in a straightforward way the kind of problem with which one has to deal in connexion with the books of the New Testament, and the way in which conclusions are reached. Some problems however are less easily resolved, and scholars may be evenly divided over them. In the case of Ephesians, for example, the arguments in favour of genuineness are strong. Many of the familiar Pauline themes and phrases known to us from other letters are found in it. It claims to be by Paul (1:1; 3:1), and has a depth and grandeur which are not usually found in the works of imitators. Unlike II Peter, it is well attested in the early second century, and was accepted as genuine from an early date. Yet there is no agreement about its authenticity, many scholars (but by no means all) holding that it is the work of an unknown Christian writing under the cover of Paul's name.

Briefly stated, the main issues are these:

(a) There was uncertainty in early times about the church to which the letter was addressed. At least one group in the second century knew it as the letter to Laodicea, and in our earliest manuscripts the words *in Ephesus* are missing from the opening verse. If Paul did write the letter, it is unlikely that he intended it for Ephesus, for he includes no greetings to individuals or references to details in the life of the church, and even assumes that his readers may not have heard of him (3:2ff), whereas Paul was well known in Ephesus (*see* Acts 20:17-31). If the letter is genuine, we must admit that we do not know the original destination. Laodicea, like Ephesus in the later manuscripts, is probably only a guess. If the letter is not genuine, however, the difficulty disappears. The address to Ephesus is intentional and its omission probably accidental.

46

(b) In many respects Ephesians is unique among the letters bearing Paul's name. It has distinctive features of vocabulary, style and teaching. For some scholars these differences are incompatible with Pauline authorship. Others argue that all great minds are capable of adapting their ideas and ways of expression to new circumstances and insights, but they admit that time would be needed for this, and they consequently place Ephesians among the last of Paul's letters, written at the end of an interval after the others.

(c) Ephesians is remarkably similar to Colossians. While it is not a slavish copy, a careful comparison of the original Greek shows that there are few sentences in the six chapters of Ephesians which do not echo a word or phrase in Colossians, although often with a new twist of meaning, or in different connexions. Those who uphold Pauline authorship argue that Colossians was fresh in his mind when he wrote Ephesians, for he is unlikely deliberately to have copied one of his own letters. Those who reject this argue that the similarities suggest an imitator using Colossians as a model.

(d) The relationship to Colossians is really the decisive issue. Many scholars find it impossible to reconcile the argument in (b), that Paul wrote Ephesians some time after Colossians, and that in (c), that he wrote while Colossians was still fresh in his mind; so they conclude on these grounds that Ephesians must be the work of an imitator. On the other side it is urged that an imitator as intellectually mature and imaginative as the writer of Ephesians has shown himself to be would hardly have needed to base himself so closely on Colossians, although this may not take sufficient account of the desire of the imitator to represent the apostle's ideas rather than his own.

The issues are thus finely balanced, and we lack the criteria in this case for a decisive judgement. No one, whichever side he takes, is entitled to feel as confident in his view of Ephesians as of II Peter or a generally accepted Pauline letter like Romans.

Not all our problems about the books of the New Testament relate to questions of authorship and date. The difficulties may concern the reconstruction of the events which necessitated writing, identifying the readers for whom the work was originally intended, or the question whether it was composed in its present form or was made up from a number of works which were perhaps available to the editor only in a fragmentary state. We know, for example, that Paul wrote more letters to Corinth than the two we have now. It is often argued, however, that not all of this additional correspondence has been lost, fragments of it being preserved in I and II Corinthians themselves. On the basis of contradictions between various sections of the letter, many hold that II Corinthians is composed of parts of two or three letters. Some have also argued for a similar view of the first letter. Those who disagree insist that such contradictions can be accounted for by the character of Paul himself, without recourse to theories of the combination of fragments. They also point to the difficulty of proposing any analysis into sources which is completely free of objection or which offers an adequate explanation for the way the sources have been combined into the letters as we now have them.

Research into these questions is of necessity very detailed, and it would require a separate volume to do justice to them. In the nature of the case generalizations can be misleading (for example one recent writer, J. A. T. Robinson, has argued against the weight of majority opinion that all the New Testament was written before AD 70) but the following brief summary may nevertheless help to provide the reader with a framework for what is discussed in later chapters of this book and form a starting point for further studies.

Of the letters of Paul four are generally accepted as genuine: Romans, I and II Corinthians, and Galatians; most would add to these Philippians, I Thessalonians and Philemon. In the case not only of I and II Corinthians but also of Philippians and the end of Romans, there is the possibility that we have the combination of originally separate letters. The authenticity of three letters is widely challenged – Colossians, II Thessalonians and Ephesians – but in no case is the issue clear-cut. In Britain the tendency is to accept the first two, while opinion is divided over the third. The so-called 'pastoral epistles', I and II Timothy and Titus, are regarded by the majority as not written by Paul, at least in their present form.

With Paul's letters our task is made easier by having so many to compare with each other. With the other epistles we are at a disadvantage in having only one or two from an author's pen, and less information about many of the authors anyway. There are some scholars who still maintain that James and Jude were written by brothers of Jesus, and I Peter by the apostle, but probably the majority regard some or all of these letters as inauthentic. Very few indeed, as we have seen, would now claim apostolic authorship for II Peter. It is generally also agreed that the ancient attribution of Hebrews to Paul is an error. The true identity of the author is probably irrecoverable. Apart from the title (added later), the work does not state his name.

The authorship of the three letters attributed to John is best considered alongside the gospel and Revelation. Their relationship is a tangled problem. Revelation claims to have been written by one named John, but few would regard him as the author of the gospel and letters because of differences of style and content. There are greater similarities between the gospel and the letters, but it is not clear whether they were written by the same individual, or were produced by a group of like-minded associates. The last two letters claim to be by 'the presbyter' but give no name; the first letter and the gospel do not indicate their authors. The gospel refers to 'the disciple whom Jesus loved', probably (but not certainly) intending John the son of Zebedee, and some would argue on this basis for some influence, however remote, by that apostle on the gospel. However, few would claim him as the direct author of any of the works which now go under the name of John.

Of the other gospels, it is very commonly denied that Matthew wrote the first gospel, and often questioned whether the attribution of the second to John Mark or the third to Luke the physician and companion of Paul is correct. (We shall nevertheless continue to use the traditional names for the authors of the four gospels in this book for the sake of convenience. No particular theory of their identity is thereby implied.) Much depends here, as in every case, on whether one begins from the early traditions of the church about authorship, which are strong particularly for Mark and Luke, or from the internal evidence of the gospels themselves, which give grounds for doubt. However, it is normally accepted that whoever wrote Luke's gospel wrote Acts as well.

Decisions on questions of authorship are bound up with questions of date. The genuine letters of Paul are without dispute among the earliest writings in the New Testament, composed before 62–64 (the earliest, on some theories, perhaps as early as 48) and antedating our gospels by between ten and fifty years. The other Pauline letters are likely to be at least a generation later. If genuine, I Peter was written before 68 and James before 62. Possibly other works, such as Hebrews, are as early, but all those written under an assumed name are likely to be much later. The favourite dates for the gospels are still as follows: Mark just before 70, Matthew and Luke (with Acts) 80–85, John 90–100 (although some press for a much earlier date) and for the Revelation about 96. Thus for those scholars who accept most of the epistles as genuine, over one-third of the New Testament was produced by about AD 70, within forty years of the crucifixion; while for the others most of it is to be dated in the last quarter of the century, and a few works later still. In either case two points need to be underlined. The first is that the earliest documents in the New Testament were not written until nearly twenty years – and the earliest gospel a whole generation – after the crucifixion. We shall have to consider later how that gap in time is to be bridged. The other point is that II Peter is definitely the latest document. The tendency which was common a hundred years ago to assign much of the New Testament to the second century has now been abandoned. We are dealing in the New Testament with the records of the earliest stages in the growth of the church.

Some readers will find this summary distressing. It suggests a scene of almost chaotic disagreement among supposed experts, and thus reinforces the reluctance of the layman to venture into the field at all. It also raises acute questions about biblical authority. Can we tolerate the conclusion that possibly none of the twenty-seven writings in the New Testament, with the exception of four letters of Paul, was written by the one to whom it is attributed in our printed Bibles? Is forgery consistent with inspiration? We shall conclude this chapter by looking at these two questions.

In connexion with the first question (concerning the lack of unanimity) it should be noted that, while there is disagreement over many of the conclusions, there is surprisingly little dispute about method. It is accepted that questions concerning the authorship and destination, the date and circumstances of origin of the New Testament documents cannot be given a snap answer on the basis simply of what they purport to be. Often questions arise precisely because the apparent character of a document cannot be reconciled with other facts about it. To answer such questions a complex series of tests is necessary, as our examples have shown. The text must be subjected to close scrutiny, and the evidence of the manuscripts and the reputation of the book in the ancient church taken into account. Psychological judgements about the capacity of an individual to express himself in different ways and to espouse apparently conflicting views may also be involved. As in the case of II Peter and Jude, judgements about one book may affect judgements about another. The difficulty is that the evidence is often ambiguous, and much has to depend upon the scholar's personal judgement, and the relative weight which he gives to different types of evidence.

Some attempts have been made in recent years, notably by A. Q. Morton working with several associates, to introduce greater objectivity by the use of statistical analysis based on computer tests. It has been shown that in certain classes of writing an author's style remains consistent over many years, whatever his subject. By checking features of style (e.g. sentence-length and the use of certain routine words) it can be settled whether two disputed writings come from the same hand. The attraction of this method is that it approximates to those used in the natural sciences, and does not appear to involve the scholar's personal judgement. Sentence-length and word-frequency are objective data to be measured and assessed according to recognized statistical procedures. Unfortunately, the applicability of the method to documents as short and unpolished as most of the New Testament ones is still in some doubt. In any case it provides an essentially negative test, in that it can only show whether a number of works attributed to the same author may in fact have come from the same hand. It cannot name the author. With many of the New Testament works our initial difficulty is that we do not have an undisputed sample of the author's work from which to start. Ultimately we are therefore left relying – because of the ambiguity of much of the evidence – upon scholarly judgement. This, combined with the fact (cf. below, page 137) that progress is made by questioning common assumptions, accounts for the sometimes bewildering variety of scholarly views. However, inasmuch as all scholars appeal to rational argument, the sensible response of the student is not to take flight, but to accept the point of view which he finds most convincing.

When we turn to the second question, concerning the possibility and acceptability of forgery, it is important to keep certain facts clearly in mind. First, the titles of the books as they are now printed in the New Testament cannot be relied on as original. Certainly letter-writers did not give titles to their communications, any more than they do now; these are added later when the letters are collected and published. In fact the titles vary in the manuscripts, and the most that can be reliably said of them is that they represent what the early church understood the books to be. They may be based on tradition or simply deduced from the contents of the work in question. It is to the contents rather than the title that we have to look for internal evidence about the author, and this is often less clear-cut.

Secondly, it is important to distinguish pseudonymity from anonymity. Some books of the New Testament – the gospels, Acts, Hebrews, the letters of John – do not indicate their author in the text. They are strictly anonymous, and Christian tradition alone suggests their authors' identities. In these cases the question of authorship concerns the possibility that the tradition is mistaken, but raises no problems about the authors' intentions. In the case of I and II Timothy, however, or other letters which purport to be by an apostle and carry his name and personal details in the text, we have to conclude (if they are not genuine) that they have been written by someone deliberately using the apostle's name. These are pseudonymous writings, and raise the objection of forgery. Can such works carry authority?

In some cases it may be possible to side-step the issue by arguing that the letter concerned was written by a secretary. We know that ancient authors rarely wrote their books in their own hand, and there is some evidence to suggest that on occasions they merely instructed their secretaries to write an appropriate letter along certain lines without necessarily supervising the result. The peculiarities of some New Testament letters might be explained in this way (cf. I Peter 5:12). In such cases we would have letters not written by an apostle but carrying his authority, and thus both those who deny and those who uphold apostolic authorship might be correct in different ways. But where the evidence against the genuineness includes considerations of the date and circumstances of composition, as with II Peter, such an escape from the dilemma is closed.

For some, the issue is clear-cut: if a work is pseudonymous, there was an intention on the part of the real author to deceive his readers, and this fact deprives him of all moral and spiritual authority. His work must automatically lose its canonical status on detection. Conversely it has been argued that the fact that a work has been included in the Canon implies that it cannot be pseudonymous, although this seems to credit the early church with infallibility in its judgement. It is doubtful, however, if either of these views does justice to the difference between modern and ancient ideas of authorship.

It is most important to recognize that, while today forgery is a crime, it was not so in the ancient world, and attitudes to it depended on the motive. It was not uncommon for books to be put on the market bearing a false author's name, either to gain prestige for them and boost sales, or even to discredit the person to whom they were falsely attributed. But other motives could operate, particularly with works of philosophy and religion. There was a widespread conviction in the ancient world that truth, being as ancient as creation, must have been known to the wise men of old. So it was common for philosophical writers belonging to a certain school, in which the sense of tradition was strong, to produce works under the name of the founder of the school long after his death. This was both because they believed that they were expounding his teaching and because a man so wise must have known the truth they were now setting forth, even if he had never put it in writing. From this point of view it would have been misleading to have attributed the work to any other person than the Master, and would have given it a false air of novelty.

When we review early Christian literature against this background, it becomes clear that, while some of the so-called apostolic books which the church later rejected may have been produced from ulterior motives, others were written in the genuine, if sometimes mistaken belief that they expounded true apostolic teaching. The pseudonymous writings of the New Testament come in the second category rather than the first. It is a striking fact that in every case the work is addressed to

Christians, with the aim of recalling readers to the gospel they have already received. There is no attempt to introduce novelty, or impart secrets hidden from ordinary believers, as in the case of some non-canonical works, nor is the apostle's name used for such purposes. While the exact purpose of the personal references to details in the apostle's life is not always clear, in most cases they appear to be intended to remind the readers of the apostle's calling and God-given authority, or to hold up his life as an example for the readers to follow, rather than (as some have too readily assumed) merely to make the letter look genuine.

The overriding aim, then, is to interpret the apostolic message in new circumstances, and recall the church to it. From our point of view the attempt may not have been particularly successful. The divergence from genuine teaching of the apostle may be the clue which enables us to detect the fact that a pseudonym has been used. Our question however concerns motive, and it is not a foregone conclusion that there must have been an intention to deceive, or that the first readers misunderstood what was being done. In fact, from the writer's point of view, it might have been more misleading to have used his own name, for it was not his own, but the apostle's teaching as he understood it that he was trying to set forth. From this perspective the work of these interpreters may carry its own kind of authority, and lay claim to its share of inspiration, for the signs are that it was what the church needed to hear at that time.

54

5. The Four Gospels

In the last chapter we saw how the detailed comparison of two letters could lead to the conclusion that they were related, the one being based – perhaps even copied – from the other. In considering the gospels we are driven to similar conclusions, although the evidence is more complex. In fact a major concern of gospel study is the question of sources, in the sense both of the documents on which they are based and more generally of the origins of the material they contain. In this chapter we shall be concerned primarily with the documentary question, but we shall begin with an example which will introduce us to a number of other problems as well.

The reader is advised at this point to read carefully through the accounts of the feeding of the five thousand in Matthew 14: 13-21, Mark 6:32-44, Luke 9:10-17, and John 6:1-13. He will discover that each account, while broadly similar in outline, differs both in detail and in context. Matthew's version comes after a section in which he describes the reactions to Jesus first of the inhabitants of his native village and then of King Herod. Herod fears that John the Baptist has risen from the dead. We are then told of the murder of John by Herod and of Jesus' retirement with his disciples at the news of it by boat to a desert place. Crowds of people, hearing of his departure, follow on foot, and when Jesus disembarks, he has compassion on them and heals the sick. Later in the day the disciples urge him to send the people away to get food, but he responds by telling the disciples themselves to provide it. They protest, pointing out that they have only five loaves and two fish. Jesus asks for these, orders the crowd to sit down, takes the bread (the fish are not mentioned again) and after saying grace gives it to the disciples to distribute. All the people are satisfied, and at the end twelve baskets full of fragments are collected. The number of the crowd, not counting women and children, Matthew notes, was five thousand. After the feeding Jesus compels his disciples to get into the boat again and set off, while he dismisses the crowd and goes up into the hills to pray alone. The incident of his walking on the water follows.

Mark has substantially the same account. There are some differences in the setting of it. According to him the reason for the withdrawal to a desert place is not the death of John, which is represented as having taken place some time earlier, but the fact that the disciples have just returned from a preaching and healing mission. Nevertheless the introduction to the incident in Mark is similar in that he refers to Herod's reaction to Jesus and includes the story of the Baptist's death. Similarly Mark follows the feeding with the dismissal of the disciples and crowds, the withdrawal of Jesus to pray and his subsequent walking on the water. In the narrative of the actual feeding Mark differs from Matthew especially in (a) portraying Jesus as teaching rather than healing the crowds (they are described, in Old Testament imagery, as sheep lacking a shepherd); (b) stressing that the crowds, anticipating his movements, were awaiting Jesus on his arrival by boat (Matthew is less clear on this point); (c) a dialogue between Jesus and the disciples in which they ask with some asperity whether he really expects them to go and spend large sums of money on bread; (d) a more vivid description of the crowds seated on the green grass; (e) making Jesus instruct the disciples to arrange for the seating of the crowd, and (f) the statement that fish as well as bread was distributed. Also Mark is less emphatic than Matthew that the number of five thousand in the crowd excludes women and children, although his language implies it.

Luke's version of the feeding combines features found separately in the other two. He represents Jesus as both teaching and healing the crowds. He is like Mark in including the disciples' incredulous suggestion that they should go and buy bread, and in implying (but not stressing) that only the men in the crowd were counted in the five thousand. However, both of these points are introduced at a different place in the narrative. Like Matthew, he makes no mention of the distribution of the fish. In the setting of his story, however, Luke is quite different from the other two. There is no mention of any lake. After the return of the disciples from their mission Jesus takes them aside to a city called Bethsaida. Only later, in the course of the narrative, do we learn that they are in a desert place. There is consequently no disembarkation at the beginning, nor any walking on the water afterwards. Instead Luke follows the feeding of the multitude with the story of Peter's confession of faith in Jesus, an episode which in Matthew and Mark is separated from it by two whole chapters and has a different geographical location at Caesarea Philippi. While there is an allusion to Herod's execution of the Baptist, the event is not described in this gospel at all.

John differs in both context and content. The incident follows a chapter describing events in Jerusalem. Jesus crosses the lake in a boat, although no reason for this is given, and the crowds meet him on the other side because they have already witnessed his healing powers. It is near Passover time; Jesus ascends a hill and sits down. Seeing the crowd Jesus asks Philip (in order to test him) where they should get bread to feed so many, and in words similar to those used by all the disciples in Mark, Philip protests at the cost which would be involved. Then Andrew introduces a boy with five loaves and two fish (a feature unique to John), Jesus instructs the disciples to seat the crowd (numbering five thousand men), says grace over bread and fish and himself distributes both to the people; all are satisfied. He gives orders for the remnants to be collected and it is found that there are twelve full baskets. The sequel to this incident is that the crowd try to make Jesus king, but he retires alone into the hills. Later the disciples embark and cross the lake and Jesus walks on the water to them.

We are thus dealing with four narratives similar in substance but different in detail. In their accounts of the incident itself the first three gospels agree fairly closely, while John tells the story in a different way. In context Luke is strikingly different, as is John at the beginning, although like Matthew and Mark he has the walking on the water at the end. Nevertheless they are clearly all versions of the same story. All include expressions of bewilderment on the part of the disciples at the suggestion that the crowds should be fed in the desert; this would be unintelligible if they were accounts of four different events, for the disciples could hardly continue to be puzzled each time if miraculous feedings kept taking place.

This general comparison of the four narratives can be

reinforced by detailed study of the text in Greek. Such a study is complicated by the presence of variant readings in the manuscripts of each gospel, some doubtless due to the desire of scribes to make the gospels conform to each other; but if for the sake of argument we adopt one of the standard modern printed texts and analyse the wording of each gospel, we arrive at the following facts: (a) the accounts differ in length: John's contains 198 words, Mark's 194, Matthew's 158, Luke's 156. (b) Matthew, Mark and Luke contain a remarkable number of words which are identical: 45 words occur precisely in the same form in all three gospels, and a further 12 are nearly the same (*crowd* instead of *crowds*, etc.). More are identical in two gospels: 34 in Matthew and Mark, 7 in Mark and Luke, and 14 in Matthew and Luke. Only 41 of Matthew's words, 86 of Mark's, 66 of Luke's have no exact or near parallel in the other two gospels. Mark's high number is related to his greater overall length. (c) No such close verbal parallelism exists between any of the first three gospels and John. While the basic ideas are similar, the vocabulary and sentence-structure differ and one cannot speak of 'exact parallels' at all except at very few points, such as the reference to the price of bread in Mark 6:37 and John 6:7. (d) Particularly striking is the description of the action of Jesus in blessing and breaking the bread (a common enough action at a Jewish meal). In Mark 6:41 there are twelve consecutive words exactly reproduced in Matthew and Luke, and ten more which are paralleled in one or other gospel or both. Only two of these words are exactly (and two more remotely) paralleled in John.

Some of these similarities are doubtless coincidental. There is only one word in common use in the New Testament for *bread*, or *disciple*, and a limited number of alternatives for such actions as *take*, *break* and *give*. Yet as John's gospel shows, it is possible to describe substantially the same events in different language, and the close similarity between the first three gospels coupled with their common difference from John demands some further explanation. The first three gospels must be related to each other in a way that none of them is to the fourth.

So far we have compared these narratives in terms of general context, narrative detail and actual wording. There is another aspect of their similarity to each other which is so obvious that it is easy to miss, but which is extremely important for the general study of the gospels: each version of the story has the same basic shape. Each begins with the crowd coming to Jesus, and by means of a dialogue between Jesus and one or more of the disciples stresses the problems of feeding them (the numbers involved, the cost of bread and the difficulty of obtaining it, the lateness of the hour, the remoteness of the location, etc.). The meagre resources available (five loaves and two fish) are mentioned. Nevertheless the crowds are made to sit down for a meal. Jesus' action in saying grace and distributing the food is described, and the story concludes rapidly, first with the statement that all were satisfied, then with a record of the number of baskets full of superfluous fragments, emphasizing the contrast with the small quantity available at the start. Of course, if we are right in concluding that the first three gospels are related to each other this similarity of outline is not surprising, but it is noteworthy that John also follows it.

It is still more striking to find that this basic shape also underlies the accounts of another miraculous feeding in Matthew 15:32-39 and Mark 8:1-10. Here only four thousand people are involved, and the quantities of food available at the beginning, and of fragments collected at the end, are different. Here too, Matthew and Mark are closely similar without being identical, and they agree on the general context. Mark is again the longer (122 words as compared with 101), but 59 words are identical in the two accounts and 11 more nearly so.

Modern scholars incline to the view that the feedings of the five thousand and the four thousand are alternative versions of the same story, for the reason already given that if the disciples had witnessed one feeding it is difficult to see why they should have failed to consider the possibility of a second. However, it is clear that Matthew and Mark regarded them as different events (*see* Matthew 16:9f and Mark 8:19f, where they have Jesus referring to both); so it is unlikely that they consciously modelled one account on the other. It is thus all the more interesting that the narratives of the feeding of the four thousand conform to the shape displayed by those of the five thousand: Jesus and the crowds, discussion with the disciples, the food available, seating the crowds, distribution, the satisfaction of all and the collection of the fragments.

59

In one sense this is a natural way to tell such a story. It highlights the salient features by setting the scene and then describing the problem, Jesus' action in meeting it, and the results. But it is not the only possible approach. The story is told exclusively from the point of view of Jesus and the disciples. The crowds are of course essential, but they remain somehow at a distance. (Contrast some modern attempts to re-tell the story which begin with the boy setting out from home with his bread and fish, and present the events through his eyes.) Many details which might be of interest are omitted. How did the multiplication of the bread occur? The Greek word used on some occasions (consistently in Mark) means literally that Jesus 'kept giving' the bread to the disciples. Did they move back and forth between him and the crowds? Did they at no point register surprise? Where did the baskets come from – are they simply an indication of the quantity of fragments left, or were actual baskets used? If not, how were the fragments gathered up, and what was done with them afterwards? These questions are not answered for us. The fact that these stories could have been told in other ways makes their common shape all the more remarkable.

The implications of this observation about the common shape of the stories we shall defer until the next chapter, and for the present we shall concentrate on the other similarities and differences we have noticed. What we have observed in one section is true of the four gospels as a whole: the first three are in many respects similar to each other, and all markedly different from the fourth. The feeding of the multitude is in fact one of the few extended passages where comparison between all four gospels is possible at all. The others are: the cleansing of the temple; walking on water (not in Luke); Jesus' anointing; the entry into Jerusalem; the arrest in Gethsemane; the general outline of the trial and crucifixion; and the discovery of the empty tomb. John also shares with Luke the miraculous draught of fish, and the appearance of the risen Jesus to the disciples in Jerusalem. But all these, like the feeding of the multitude, differ in John both in detail and in the context in which they are placed. In the case of the cleansing of the temple and the miraculous draught of fish the context is transferred from one end of Jesus' ministry to the other.

In many other respects John is quite different from the other three gospels. The ministry of Jesus begins, not with the call of the disciples by the lakeside after John the Baptist's imprisonment, but by the Jordan while John is still at work. Jesus does not, as in the other three gospels, visit Jerusalem only at the end of his ministry but periodically throughout it; seven-and-a-half of the first twelve chapters of the gospel are set there. Many episodes familiar to us from the other gospels are absent: the temptations, transfiguration, institution of the Lord's Supper, prayer in Gethsemane. Jesus is not described as driving out demons from the possessed, nor does he teach the crowds in parables of the kind familiar to us from the other gospels. Individual sayings in John's gospel can be compared with sayings in the other three, but generally we miss the brevity and episodic character of the teaching as they present it. The content differs too, the teaching of Jesus in John being concerned with themes not dealt with elsewhere. In John sayings and narrative alike display a common style, so that it is difficult at times in this gospel to decide whether we are reading the words of Jesus or the comment of the evangelist.

These differences have long been evident, at least since the end of the second century when it was suggested that, while the first three gospels present what were then called the material facts of the life of Jesus, the fourth gave them a spiritual interpretation. Whatever the true explanation, the differences are the basis of the fundamental distinction all scholars now draw between the first three (known as the *synoptic*) gospels and John. Opinions differ as to whether the author of the fourth gospel knew the other three; some argue that a few common phrases such as the reference to the price of bread in John 6:7 show that he was at least aware of Mark, while others consider them to be coincidental. But all agree that this gospel stands apart from the other three.

With Matthew, Mark and Luke things are different. Clearly each has its own characteristics and distinctive contents, yet all follow the same general story from the beginning of the ministry to the crucifixion and burial. In many sections there is extensive verbal similarity or even identity between all three gospels; in others, particularly sections containing teaching, the identity or similarity in wording is between Matthew and Luke, there being no parallel in Mark. The explanation of these facts has long been sought in some form of literary dependence, and for over fifty years the most widely accepted solution has been the one which was given its classic statement in English by B. H. Streeter in 1924, namely that Mark was the first gospel to be written, and that Matthew and Luke both independently used it along with a second written source (now lost) containing teaching material not used by Mark, and for convenience designated 'Q'. Matthew and Luke also each had access to material not available to the other, designated 'M' and 'L' respectively. This solution has never been universally accepted, particularly by Roman Catholic scholars who have tended until recently to support the earlier view that Matthew was the first to be written. Attempts are still made from time to time to offer alternative solutions, but Streeter's is still by far the most widely held, and forms the starting point for all further study of the gospels.

The arguments which support this solution of the 'synoptic problem' are based on a detailed word by word comparison of the three gospels of the kind which we briefly undertook for the feeding of the multitude. It is found that 90 per cent of Mark's subject matter is also contained in Matthew, more than half of it in identical words, and over 50 per cent is contained in Luke, again more than half in identical words. In individual passages where Matthew, Mark and Luke have parallel versions, as much as 60 per cent of Mark's wording may be contained in both the other two and much of the remainder may appear in one or the other (our example was not typical in this respect). Only a small proportion of the wording in such passages is identical in Matthew and Luke but not in Mark. When we turn from wording to the arrangement of the material we find that while each gospel has its own order at certain points, frequently all three agree; elsewhere we nearly always find either Matthew or Luke agreeing with Mark. Never do Matthew and Luke agree against Mark on a point of arrangement, apart from some relatively small details. These agreements in wording and order of Matthew and Luke with Mark but not with each other are best explained if we assume that they both independently used Mark as a source for their own work. This is supported by the fact that many of the particular points at which Matthew or Luke differ from Mark (in passages where they generally agree) can be explained as attempts to improve Mark's linguistic style or theological expression. Perhaps the decisive fact is that while Mark is the shortest gospel over all, in individual passages it frequently has the longest version (as in our example), not on account of the presence of significant additional material but because the story is told with fuller descriptive detail. This can be explained better on the supposition that both Matthew and Luke needed to abbreviate Mark in order to make room for other material than on the theory that Mark abbreviated one or other (or both) and then compensated for this by expanding what remained.

Similar arguments are used to support the hypothesis of the document 'Q'. There are many sections of sayings – material peculiar to Matthew and Luke – which are closely similar, either simply in content or even in actual wording. In some passages the similarity is too close and extensive to be coincidental. Further, much of this common material appears in both gospels in the same order, although not in the same contexts. These facts point to a common written source, now lost, containing sayings of Jesus from which each evangelist has drawn.

To say that this explanation of the relationships between the synoptic gospels is the one most frequently adopted is not to suggest that it is free of difficulties. It is upon such difficulties that critics tend to fasten, and although no alternative explanation so far offered has won any wide measure of support the difficulties remain. The most glaring of these is the relatively small number of cases where Matthew and Luke agree in wording against Mark in a passage where otherwise they appear to be following him. Some of these occurred in our sample passage of the feeding of the five thousand. The normal way of dealing with them is to suggest either that they are coincidental (being modifications which might naturally suggest themselves to an evangelist working on the text of Mark) or that they are the result of subsequent attempts by scribes to harmonize the text of one gospel with another in the normal process of copying. Sometimes it is suggested that the version of Mark which we now have is a slightly later edition than the one used by Matthew and Luke, so that their common wording in these passages may after all have been derived from the Mark which they saw. These lines of approach are usually adopted because they represent the lesser of two evils, the greater being to deny the priority of Mark and then to try to explain away the evidence in its favour, but it is doubtful whether any sensitive scholar is altogether at ease about this problem.

Another difficulty in the theory that Mark was the earliest gospel is the fact that one would expect it consistently to offer the most 'primitive' version of a story or saying; that is, the version which could most easily be translated back into the Aramaic dialect which Jesus probably spoke, or which reflected Palestinian rather than Greek or Roman conditions of life, or which was otherwise comparatively free from obviously later embellishment. This is not always the case. For example, in Mark 10:2-12 rulings are given on divorce which, in forbidding a woman to divorce her husband, reflect Gentile practice, for under Jewish law such a possibility was not envisaged. As the point of the passage is to emphasize that the standard Jesus sets is more rigorous than the provisions of the Mosaic law, it is hard to see why Jesus should specially forbid his Jewish hearers to do something for which the law did not in fact make provision. However it would make sense for such a point to be emphasized in a Gentile environment, perhaps in Rome, where Mark's gospel may have been written, and where such a practice might need to be specially forbidden for readers accustomed to the laxer provisions of Roman law. If this is so, we have a case of the adaptation of the sayings of Jesus to draw out their implications for a different situation, a possibility to which we shall return later. In Matthew 19:3-12, however, which according to Streeter's theory was based on Mark (and is certainly closely parallel to it), the wording reflects the Jewish situation which must have obtained in Jesus' time; no mention is made of a woman initiating a divorce. The allegedly secondary gospel is thus at this point the more 'primitive'. Such cases are not very numerous, certainly not sufficient by themselves to overthrow the general hypothesis that Mark was the earliest gospel; but they do pose important and difficult questions about the reasons why one gospel should differ from another, and about the sources of the variant material which has been introduced.

A third difficulty concerns 'Q'. A basic difference between the theory of the priority of Mark and that concerning Q is that while we still possess Mark, Q according to the hypothesis no longer exists and must be reconstructed out of the texts of Matthew and Luke. Herein lies the difficulty. While there are certainly passages which are so closely similar that it is difficult to believe that they can be explained by anything less than a common written source in Greek, these are combined with other passages where the subject matter is similar but the wording, for no apparent reason, very different. Both categories of passages are attributed in the Q-hypothesis to a single document, because they occur in the same order in both Matthew and Luke. But why should one of the evangelists have altered his source so radically in some passages but not in others? Is the common order of these passages so decisive? Many scholars would now question whether it is. For example: they would not argue that extracts of John the Baptist's teaching and details of the temptations occur at the beginning of Jesus' ministry in both Matthew and Luke because they stood at the beginning of an extended sayings-collection upon which the two evangelists regularly drew. Rather they would say that the gospel of Mark (which both were following) refers to the Baptist and to the temptation at the beginning of the ministry, and so provided the natural contexts into which this material could be inserted. The two sets of parallel material in Matthew and Luke may each have come from common sources, but not necessarily both from the same source.

Thus it may be that the material commonly designated Q should more correctly be attributed to a variety of sources. While the closely parallel passages may have been taken from one or more written documents containing sayings of Jesus in Greek, some of the other sections may have come to Matthew and Luke either from an Aramaic source which they independently translated or from different sources, the similarities being due to their common origin in the teaching of Jesus. For these reasons the symbol Q is often used today simply as a convenient way of referring to those passages which are common to Matthew and Luke without implying any particular theory about their origin.

One aspect of Streeter's theory about which he himself had clear views but which has never been satisfactorily settled is the question how Luke used his sources. Matthew and Luke adopt different methods in their use of Mark. While Matthew tends to interweave all his sources – Mark, Q and M – together, Luke appears to follow Mark alone for an extended section, and then switch to a section in which Q and L only are combined, before reverting to Mark again. On the basis of this Streeter and others argued that Luke had already prepared a gospel before he came across Mark, which he used by inserting sections into his draft at points where he felt it to be most lacking. While this 'Proto-Luke' theory has appeared attractive to some, it is difficult to prove. Because Luke is rather freer than Matthew in his treatment of Mark's language, it is not always clear whether he is freely adapting Mark or following an independent source. This is particularly so in the story of the trial and death of Jesus. On the whole the trend at present is probably rather against Streeter's theory, for reasons which will become clear later (page 102).

The 'generally accepted solution' is thus not without its difficulties, but it is still widely preferred as giving the most reliable explanation of the facts. If it is true, it tells us much about the sources of Matthew and Luke and gives us an important insight into the way in which these gospels were composed. It shows that their authors were not freely composing, but reproducing material composed by others for which they felt some respect. Two questions however are left unanswered by it. On the one hand, while scholars sometimes refer to the 'four document hypothesis' as though not only Mark and Q but also M and L were written sources, in fact the theory offers us little solid information about the character of the material in Matthew and Luke not derived from Mark or Q. From this point of view the alternative term, 'two document hypothesis', which asserts the written character only of Mark and Q (other sources being assumed to be oral), is a more satisfactory description. Nor does the theory say anything about the basis upon which Mark's gospel was composed. Was this also based upon written sources which have since perished?

The other unanswered question was indeed not consciously posed as such by many scholars until more recent years: why do Matthew and Luke modify the material they take over from Mark? We have suggested that they abbreviated Mark's narrative in order to leave space for further material, and that at places they tried to improve Mark's style or to amend theologically infelicitous statements (thus: 'he could do no mighty works

66

there' in Mark 6:5 becomes 'he did not do many mighty works there' in Matthew 13:58, thereby avoiding the suggestion that Jesus' power was limited). But these hardly seem to be sufficient explanations for all the facts. Why in our example did Luke omit not only the miracle of the walking on the water but all reference to the lake in connexion with the feeding of the multitude, and locate the event at Bethsaida, thereby creating an incongruity with the reference to a desert place? Why did Matthew, in both feeding stories, add to what he took from Mark the statement that the number of the crowd did not include women and children? What were the aims of the gospel writers; what in fact is a gospel? The answer to such questions will emerge in the following chapters.

6. Behind the Written Word - 1

When we were considering the six narratives of Jesus' feeding of the multitudes in the last chapter, we noticed two features upon which we deferred comment: the variation in the contexts in which the stories are set; and the identity of basic shape which all the versions possess. Wider study shows that these features are common throughout the synoptic gospels.

Even where he is closely following Mark in wording Matthew frequently rearranges the sequence of passages, particularly in the first half of his gospel; for example, by spreading the contents of Mark's second chapter over chapters 9 and 12, and introducing earlier in chapter 8 episodes from Mark 4 and 5. Luke does not do this to the same extent, although his arrangement in chapters 6 to 8 (where he uses material from Mark 3 and 4 with some variation of order and a long insertion of other material in the middle) illustrates a similar technique; and we have already noted his completely different context for the feeding in chapter 9 (*see* p. 56). Clearly neither Matthew nor Luke regarded Mark's framework as sacrosanct; both felt free to rearrange it and to introduce additional material, although as we saw it was a major argument for Streeter's solution of the synoptic problem that Matthew and Luke do not agree against Mark on a point of order. The significant point is that the material lends itself to this kind of treatment; it is episodic in character. The evangelists were able to work with units, brief samples of teaching, or single narratives of a healing, or an encounter between Jesus and opponents. These units are often only loosely connected, by such phrases as 'and it came to pass that . . .', and are capable of arrangement in different ways, each being intelligible by itself without reference to what comes before or after. Only in the story of Jesus' passion and death do we have a long sequence of episodes where the sequence itself is important and each episode depends for its significance on what precedes and follows it. Nevertheless even here there are variations in order between the gospels. The synoptic gospels, in other words, dissolve into self-contained portions, much as the demolition of a house leaves not a pile of dust but a heap of bricks which can be reassembled into a new building.

Further, as in the case of the feeding narratives, when these units are compared one with another it is found that they tend to conform to general patterns; the bricks, so to speak, turn out to be of a limited number of standard designs. This is true not only of parallel versions of the same incident in different gospels but of different passages within the same gospel which do not have the same content. In the last fifty years much attention has been given to this fact, and a branch of New Testament study – known as form criticism – developed to deal with it. In this chapter we shall try to illustrate what form criticism is and discuss some of the problems connected with it.

Form criticism begins by classifying the units of material (or *pericopae*) in the gospels according to their form. Four main groups are usually identified. The names given to them vary somewhat in different writers, but those used here are common in English works and will serve as a general guide.

The first group consists of the *miracle stories*, of which the feeding of the multitude is an example, although the majority describe healings or the expulsion of demons. Certain elements tend to recur, some of which we have already observed. The nature of the problem is stated, e.g. the gravity and duration of the illness, the failure of doctors or disciples, the anxiety or fear of bystanders, the plight of the crowd in late evening in a desert place with hopelessly inadequate food. Then the action of Jesus, his gesture or word as in blessing and breaking the bread, is described. The success of his action is shown, e.g. by the sick man getting up, by the evidence of the demon departing, or by the quantity of food left over. Frequently a note is added of the impression made upon bystanders, their awe and amazement. The focus of the story is always the action of Jesus in meeting the need, and this is combined with a marked economy of narrative. Few details are given which are not essential to the main point. How little we are told, for example, about Peter's wife's mother except that Jesus healed her!

A second group consists of *pronouncement stories*. In episodes of this type a brief story leads up to a short, memorable saying

69

of Jesus. The occasion of the saying may be an action of Jesus or his disciples which is attacked (e.g. plucking and rubbing grain on the sabbath, in Mark 2:23-28), or a question which is asked, (as 'Is it lawful to pay tribute?' in Mark 12:13-17). The questioners may be hostile as in both these instances, or sympathetic as in the case of the rich man (Mark 10:17-22). The interest of the episode lies entirely in the saying which provides the climax; other details are introduced only in so far as they are necessary to make the saying intelligible. Only rarely does the story go on to say what happened after Jesus had spoken, and then usually only to state that his interlocutors were speechless. Events are of interest only as background to the saying.

A third category consists of *sayings of Jesus* which lack such narrative backing. Some are prefaced by the phrase *and he said to his disciples* or simply *and he said*; many have no introduction at all. Nothing in the saying itself describes the circumstances in which it was uttered. This is suggested only by the position it is given in the gospel, its connexion with other sayings or narratives. But the freedom with which the evangelists allocate the sayings to different contexts (much greater in respect of this group of material than the others), shows that originally they were entirely independent. Many of the sayings of the Sermon on the Mount, for example, have parallels in quite different contexts in Luke.

Of course within this category there is a wide variety of sayings from extended parables to single sentences Some sub-groups can be formed which conform to particular patterns, such as *if anyone . . . let him . . .* (Mark 8:34), *whosoever . . . he shall be . . .* (Matthew 5:19), *you have heard . . . but I say . . .* (Matthew 5:27f). Then there are the short proverbial sayings like 'Where the corpse is, there the vultures gather' (Luke 17:37) or longer story-parables like that of the sower. A recurring feature of many sayings, and an important criterion in discussing their origin, is the possibility of translating them back from the Greek of the New Testament into the Aramaic language which Jesus probably spoke, and discovering that they conform to the general rules governing poetic form in that language, both in containing a regular rhythm – two, three, or four beats to a line – and in using devices such as alliteration, and 'antithetic parallelism' (in which an idea is stated twice, positively and negatively, in successive lines, e.g. Matthew 6:14f). In this group, as in the previous two, the stress is on what is really essential. What is preserved is the saying of Jesus, not the occasion on which he said it, still less incidentals such as the time of day or the state of the weather.

The fourth group covers what remains, more general *stories about Christ*, which because of their variety cannot easily be reduced to a standard pattern. The stories of his baptism and temptation, the call of the disciples, the transfiguration, and the entry into Jerusalem are to be included here, as are many parts of the story of the passion and resurrection. Once again it is appropriate to draw attention to the economy of the material. In contrast to some Old Testament stories, there is little here of the story-teller's love of detail or tendency to drag the narrative out in order to heighten the climax. These stories are short and to the point: Jesus sees men mending nets or collecting taxes; he commands, and they obey instantly and without question, leaving everything in order to follow. The soldiers lead Jesus out, pressing Simon of Cyrene to carry his cross, and crucify him. How much detail is omitted!

So underlying the diversity of contents in the first three gospels can be discerned many similarities of form, and we have noticed common to all types an economy of detail, a single-mindedness which concentrates on certain essentials. How is this to be explained? These features cannot be attributed to the style of individual writers, for they are to be found in all three synoptic gospels. Nor can they be explained simply as characteristics of the teaching of Jesus himself, for they are to be found in narratives about him as well. Only oral tradition will account for them, and a particular kind of oral tradition at that.

The point can best be illustrated by contrast. If we invite an old man to tell us about some incident which occurred in his youth, but which he has not recalled for many years, the result is likely to be a rather rambling story, with a number of false starts, repetitions and blind alleys. He will tell us far more than we need to know. Some have thought of the gospels in these terms. Of course Jesus did not write a book, and any knowledge we have of his teaching and activity must depend ultimately on those who saw and heard him. Early church traditions speak of the reminiscences of Peter on which Mark's gospel was believed to be based, and the picture is conjured up of the eager young evangelist interrogating eyewitnesses about Jesus before they grew too old to remember clearly. A reason which has been suggested for the writing of the gospels was to preserve for posterity the memories of the eyewitnesses who were beginning to die off. Whatever part eyewitnesses may have played in the process, the gospels do not contain reminiscences of this kind. Their stereotyped forms and economy of detail point to frequent repetition. As experience shows, any account of an event is more economically told every time it is repeated, until it is pared down to essentials.

There is one exception to this. Stories told for their entertainment value, like jokes and fairy tales, tend to grow longer. Repetition and embellishment add to the fun. There are stories of this type in the Old Testament, in the later apocryphal gospels, and in some of the parables, but in general the contrast with the synoptic gospels is most marked. These stories are told with a seriousness of purpose which determines what shall be included and what omitted. They are instruments of teaching and preaching.

The formal characteristics of the gospel material therefore point to its origin in oral tradition; that is, it was passed on by word of mouth, frequently repeated and drawn upon. The episodic character of the material points in the same direction. In oral teaching and preaching, for the most part only isolated sayings and stories are needed on a given occasion. The main exception to this would be the story of Jesus' death, which would need to be told – at least in outline – as a connected whole.

This conclusion is fundamental to form criticism. Even though we have argued that Matthew and Luke at least drew on written sources (Mark and Q), at an earlier stage all the material was oral and bears the marks of the fact.

Moreover this conclusion is confirmed by a closer look at the way the material under the title of the sayings of Jesus is arranged. Although we have argued that the sayings were originally handed on as separate items, as we now have them short sayings are often collected together into longer paragraphs, sometimes attached to a pronouncement story. While in some cases a link of subject-matter is obvious, in others the arrangement is somewhat artificial, depending on the recurrence of a word (not necessarily with the same meaning every time) rather than on any real connexion of sense. The classic passage for this is Mark 9:33-50, where, particularly at the end of the paragraph, sayings appear to be linked simply by the fact that they contain such words as *in the name, offend, fire* and *salt*. The use of catchwords is common in oral tradition at all times, as an aid to memory in the absence of written notes, and this appears to be the explanation in Mark 9:33ff. The arrangement of pronouncement stories and sayings in this paragraph is due not to the writer of the gospel nor simply to their having been connected from the beginning, for some are differently distributed in the other gospels. It is due to those who, at the stage of oral tradition, were already building up longer sections of teaching out of individual sayings. The same may be true in other places in the gospels, as we shall see.

Further confirmation of our conclusion can be found elsewhere in the New Testament. Paul on two occasions reminds his readers of information about Jesus which he had previously given to them (I Corinthians 11:23; 15:1-3). One passage contains a summary statement of the facts about Jesus' death and resurrection appearances, the other a narrative about the Last Supper told, as in the gospels, as an independent episode. In both cases Paul refers to what he had himself *received* and later *handed on*, terms appropriate to oral tradition. He also occasionally refers to sayings of Jesus, but never in the precise form in which they occur in the gospels (I Corinthians 7:10 – cf. Mark 10:9; I Corinthians 9:14 – cf. Luke 10:7; I Thessalonians 4:15f). Presumably these too came to him from oral tradition and he used them in his teaching and letters as and when he needed them.

The importance of this conclusion should not be missed. It helps to fill the gap between the writing of the gospels and the events to which they refer, a period of nearly forty years in the case of Mark, longer in the case of Matthew and Luke. How dependable would memory be, so long after the crucifixion? Form criticism enables us to see how the traditions had been kept alive during the interval by continuous use. There is no need to think of a 'black-out period' when the early church passed out of contact with the events upon which it was based.

This may seem a surprising conclusion in view of the fact that the work of the early form critics was viewed with much suspicion in other parts of the scholarly world and beyond its borders precisely because they tended to assume that very little of the gospels could be traced back with any probability to Jesus himself. Most of the stories about him were to be regarded as the product of sanctified imagination; even the few sayings which went back to him were much worked over by the Christians who handed them on; many were entirely creations of the Christian community. While it is probably fair to say that most modern practitioners of form criticism are not so sceptical in this regard as the great pioneer, Rudolf Bultmann, they would still adopt a very cautious attitude to the genuineness of the contents of the gospels.

We shall be in a better position later on to appreciate part of the reason why this view has been taken. The main point however is the variation to which oral tradition is prone. This can be illustrated from the gospels themselves and from the comparatively scanty records in later Christian writers of sayings of Jesus which continued to circulate in oral tradition even after the written gospels were in use. We have just seen that Paul never quotes a saying of Jesus in its precise gospel form. We have many examples in the gospels of sayings which are similar enough to invite the suspicion that they are variant forms of one original. In some cases of course Jesus himself may have been responsible for the variants; it is arbitrary to assume that he never repeated himself in different words. But this cannot explain all the variants. Apart from the fact that some inspire greater confidence in their genuineness than others because they are more easily translated back into Aramaic, are we to assume, for example, that at his trial the high priest put to Jesus three times the same question in almost, but not quite, identical terms, and that he replied each time in a slightly different way, with the fortunate outcome that each gospel has preserved one-third of the whole conversation? (see Matthew 26:63f, Mark 14:61f, Luke 22: 67-9.)

Whether we attribute the variations between the gospels to the evangelists or to their predecessors in oral tradition, it is difficult to escape the conclusion – which any acquaintance with oral tradition in modern life would lead one to expect – that the spoken word lacks the fixity of writing. Rumours spread and grow; accounts of real events become garbled. What is handed on is often not the precise account as heard, but its substance, or what is believed by the hearer to be its substance. At every stage there is the danger of distortion. Still more disturbing is the fact that traditions can arise which are unfounded.

Various arguments have been brought forward in the attempt to resist this conclusion.

(1) It has been pointed out that in societies which rely on writing less than we do, memories are more retentive and more accurate. This can be shown by many examples, e.g. of illiterate Muslims who are able to recite the whole Koran by heart.

(2) It has also been argued that the form critics ignore the presence of eye-witnesses in the church. Would not those who had been present at the time, and remembered what Jesus had said and done, have acted as a check on the tradition? Doubtless they would, if we may assume that they were all equally endowed with accurate memories. But how widely were these eye-witnesses scattered? Apart from a limited number of disciples who acted as the first missionaries, but of whose activities we have in most cases no further knowledge, most of the witnesses of Jesus' ministry will have been Galileans who never left home. Yet the form critic's case, as we shall see, is that many of the modifications occurred in Christian communities in other parts of the ancient world, where no eye-witnesses were available for consultation. In any case, the form critic asks, how are we to distinguish those parts of the gospels which are guaranteed by eye-witnesses and those which are not?

(3) A third line of argument has been developed by some Scandinavian scholars, notably H. Riesenfeld and B. Gerhardsson. In their view Jesus is best understood on the analogy of Jewish rabbis who deliberately taught their disciples set-pieces to remember by heart and pass on to others in turn. They claim that the poetic structure of much of the teaching of Jesus shows that it was designed to be learned by heart and we can therefore assume a greater degree of accuracy in the sayings of Jesus than we should expect from other forms of oral tradition. There may be some truth in this, as the gospels do depict Jesus as a teacher with disciples (although not only as this), but if it were true the argument would apply only to the sayings of Jesus and not to

75

the stories about him. It is disputed however how far the analogy between Jesus and the rabbis ought to be pressed. This argument, like the first, really founders on the fact that the New Testament itself shows that while the fluidity of oral tradition at that time and in those circumstances can certainly be over-emphasized, variations in the tradition did occur.

The implications of this discussion for our historical knowledge of Jesus himself will be considered in chapter 9. The point at the moment is that it is nevertheless still true to say that recognition of the place of oral tradition behind the gospels gives us cause for greater confidence, not less, than we should have if we were able to regard them only as belated efforts to recall a distant past or, still worse, as sheer fiction; for the aim of tradition, whatever its success in the endeavour, is always to preserve.

This conservatism is an important factor in the passage we are now going to study. Form criticism is concerned not only with classifying the contents of the gospels and demonstrating their originally oral character, but with charting their growth. The following paragraphs will illustrate this in practice, and incidentally show how form criticism contributes to our understanding of a passage which otherwise remains obscure.

Luke 16 consists of two parables, the unjust steward (NEB: 'bailiff') and the rich man and Lazarus, separated by a series of short sayings. The first part is addressed to disciples (verses 1-13), the second to Pharisees (verses 15-31) in reply to their reaction to the first part which they have overheard (verse 14). Commentators have often found difficulty in tracing any close connexion of ideas in this chapter. Particular difficulty attaches to the abrupt reference to divorce in verse 18.

The form critic will begin with the recognition that the chapter is not a verbatim record of two speeches given by Jesus on a single occasion but a collection of originally separate sayings which have subsequently been brought together. Some of them have parallels in different contexts in other gospels. There is no difficulty therefore in acknowledging the lack of continuity in the thought. The sayings are unconnected and were originally uttered at different times and in a variety of contexts which have since been forgotten. Nevertheless they now stand together in one chapter and some reason must be sought for this. At this point help is gained from the realization that the chapter was not assembled at a single stage but was built up gradually by addition over a period.

We begin with the parable of the bailiff; our approach to the parables of Jesus was revolutionized in 1888 by A. Jülicher, who argued that a distinction should be drawn between parable and allegory. In allegory every detail in the story has a symbolic significance: a parable has just one point, the details being included only for the sake of the realism of the story. Jesus taught in parables, although for many centuries Christian commentators (including the writers of the gospels) have treated them as allegories. Most modern scholars have accepted Jülicher's main contention, although some now argue (perhaps rightly) that he overstated it and some allegorical elements cannot be eliminated from the parables in their original form.

If we approach the parable of the bailiff from this point of view we may consider that, although the story concerns the behaviour of a household bailiff or estate manager, the original point of the parable had nothing to do with money, but concerned the way the man reacted in the face of a crisis in his life. The parable urged its hearers to do as the bailiff had done: faced with an imminent crisis in their lives, God's impending judgement, they too should act resolutely to prepare themselves. It was a call for repentance. Originally it ended at verse 7, without further comment, making its point by the story alone as the parables of Jesus usually do.

The two parts of verse 8 now begin to make more sense. They did not belong to the parable as originally told, but were the Christian narrator's comments upon it. The 'master' here (literally *lord*) is not the rich man in the parable, who could hardly have been pleased with the bailiff's conduct, but Jesus (compare Luke 18:6). As the parable was repeated, Jesus' intention in telling it was explained. He praised the man in the parable for acting 'astutely', because faced with the threat of disaster he took resolute action.

In the process there was a change of audience. The most obvious audience in the ministry of Jesus for an appeal to repent, we may think, was the crowd listening to his preaching, or possibly some of his opponents, particularly if Mark 4:33f is correct in suggesting that parables belonged primarily to his

77

public teaching rather than to his work with his disciples. But in the subsequent use of the parable in Christian preaching the audience is the congregation in the church. This was certainly the case in the second half of verse 8, where the appeal is made to Christians (the 'sons of light') who so often seem to show less common sense in matters spiritual than the avowedly ungodly in their line of business. To this change of audience the beginning of the parable is to be attributed, 'he said to his disciples'.

At a later stage there was a shift in meaning. The parable came to be used not as an appeal for repentance but as a warning about the use of money, and other sayings were added one by one as a commentary to bring out the new meaning. The new interpretation was hard to reconcile with verse 8, but this verse was not removed, as it was by now felt to be part of the parable. Verse 9 draws a moral from the parable based not on the way the bailiff acted but on what he did. As through the medium of money he made friends who would care for him afterwards, so the disciples are bidden to use money in such a way that they find a friend in God who, when earthly things pass away, will receive them into his heavenly dwelling. (So the rather obscure wording should probably be interpreted; it is a call to generosity and almsgiving, cf. Luke 12:33.) Verses 10-12 carry forward this theme in more general terms: faithfulness with money qualifies a man to handle eternal treasure; and verse 13 (cf. Matthew 6:24) on a rather different note adds a warning about having only one master. We note how the repetition of the word 'mammon' in verses 9, 11 and 13 binds the section together. Perhaps it was this catchword which, acting like a magnet, helped to draw the additional sayings to the parable, each giving the parable a fresh application.

In verses 14-15 the Pharisees are introduced. The teaching of the previous chapter had already been directed against them (15:2). Their love of money and self-righteousness are mentioned. This naturally leads on to mention of the law, on which their self-righteousness is based. The law and the prophets belong to the time before Jesus: from this time onward the good news of God's kingdom is proclaimed. Yet the law retains its validity. As the following parable will show, the law and the prophets contain a call to repentance which men must heed (verses 16-17, cf. verses 29-31). So the way is prepared for the parable of the rich man and Lazarus, which attacks the self-righteous indifference of the rich. What then of verse 18? We note that there is a parallel to this verse in Matthew 5:32, in a context similar to that provided by verse 17 of Luke. In Matthew 5:17-48 the point is made in a number of ways that Jesus has not come to abolish the law of Moses but to uphold it. He goes behind the qualifications and exceptions which men have imposed upon it, to its original intention, illustrating the point with reference to murder (Matthew 21-26), adultery (verses 27-30), divorce (verses 31f), perjury (verses 33-37), revenge (verses 38-42) and love (verses 43-48). Thus Matthew 5:32 is one of a series of illustrations of Matthew 5:18. At some stage before Luke took them over, his verses 17 and 18 must have served the same purpose; verse 18 illustrated the permanence of the law stated in verse 17, just as verse 32 in Matthew 5 illustrated verse 18. But in the context of his chapter 16 Luke has used verse 17 for a quite different purpose, to show the permanence of the law in calling men to repentance, and to introduce verses 19ff. But as verse 18 had become attached to it in oral tradition he includes it, although in its new setting it breaks the sequence of thought.

Whether or not this analysis of Luke 16 is correct in all its details, it illustrates the methods employed by form criticism. In practice form criticism includes much more than a study of form. On the one hand it includes questions of content, for consistency of meaning has been an important factor in our analysis, while on the other hand it broadens out into a general study of the history of the traditions in the gospels (and is sometimes known, in consequence, as the *traditio-historical method*). It offers an explanation for apparent contradictions in terms of successive stages in the development of the tradition, with each new stage, like the successive layers uncovered by an archaeological dig, resting upon its predecessor and modifying it, while leaving it essentially undisturbed for the critic to study.

In this way form criticism becomes a tool for the study of the history of the church. Earlier in this chapter we drew attention to the economy of the traditions about Jesus in their selection of certain details, and the seriousness of purpose which lies behind them. This selection tells us much about those who preserved the traditions, for the points which are highlighted show the purposes for which the stories were told. The teaching and preaching interests which it was intended to serve are revealed in the way the material is shaped. The debates between Jesus and the Pharisees, for instance, are likely to reflect current conflicts between Christians and their critics. They were recounted because they preserved the Lord's pronouncement upon living issues. This factor, indeed, must account not only for the form of what has been preserved, but for its preservation at all. Much that we should like to know about Jesus has been lost to us, because the early Christians saw no reason to recall it and pass it on. What we do have we owe to its serviceableness in the life of the church before the gospels were written. Thus from the contents of the gospels and their forms we can reconstruct some of the concerns of the early church, and an important part of the form critic's task is to try to establish the setting-in-life or *Sitz im Leben* of the material (that is, the place it had in the life of the church which used it) and so to extend our knowledge of the church in its formative period. (One of the ways by which New Testament scholars attempt, like doctors, to maintain the mystique of their profession is by the use – to the constant irritation of the non-specialist – of untranslated technical terms in foreign languages, in this case German.)

But the form critic, like any archaeologist, likes whenever possible to go still further and fix the date of the various layers he has uncovered. Of course he lacks the background information in all but a few instances for doing this in terms of years in the calendar. He can however attempt to identify the different stages in the development of the church at which the layers were formed and the influences which brought them about.

A common method employed is to identify the cultural group represented in the Christian community responsible for a particular feature in the tradition. Were they Jewish or Gentile Christians? Did they speak Aramaic or Greek? Thus it is common to find references in studies of the early church to Palestinian and Hellenistic communities or, to use a more refined set of categories, Palestinian Jewish, Hellenistic Jewish and Hellenistic.

Inevitably certain assumptions are involved here. One is that it is possible to differentiate between such groups. Indeed we know that there were differences of outlook and ideas between

Jews in Judaea and Galilee and their brothers in other parts of the Roman Empire. The latter commonly spoke Greek, and read the Old Testament in that language; most of the former did not use Greek. More obviously there were differences between Jews and Gentiles. It is likely that such differences would be reflected within the church. A clear example is the way in which the word *Christ*, which is the Greek equivalent of the Hebrew *Messiah*, gradually lost its meaning as the title of the expected Jewish ruler and became simply a second name for Jesus, as the church became more predominantly Gentile without any understanding of, or interest in Jewish national aspirations. Although these distinctions are obvious up to a point, what is less clear is whether we know enough about them to serve as a basis for stating definitely that a saying of Jesus betrays the interests of one group rather than another and must therefore have originated there.

A second assumption which accompanies the first is that the picture of the missionary expansion of the church, derived from Acts, by which it spread first among Jews in Jerusalem then among Jews elsewhere and eventually to Gentiles, entitles us to arrange these cultural groupings in order of antiquity. The Palestinian Jewish Christians would then be the earliest, the (Gentile) Hellenistic Christians the latest group to emerge. Often this is accompanied by the further tacit assumption that each group replaced another, so that a tradition bearing Palestinian Jewish characteristics must be earlier than one bearing Hellenistic Jewish characteristics. This assumption is precarious. We know that a Jewish Christian community survived in Jerusalem almost until the city was captured by the Romans in AD 70. By this time there must have been many congregations in other parts of the world which were predominantly if not entirely Hellenistic. All three types must have come into existence very early, and a so-called Hellenistic Jewish trait may therefore historically be older than a Palestinian Jewish one.

Often a third assumption is employed. This is that we already know enough about the development of Christian doctrine and church order in the decades before any part of the New Testament was written to pronounce with certainty that certain ideas or practices must be early or late. It is thus often assumed that an expectation of the Lord's return to earth in the first days

81

after the resurrection gradually gave way to an outlook which pushed this expectation on to the periphery. In general terms this may well be true (see above, page 40), but this does not entitle us to conclude that the development was consistent and uniform in every part of the church.

Thus the form critic's efforts to date his layers of evidence are often frustrated by lack of precise information. Nevertheless it is a legitimate quest, for the effort to understand anything from the past involves setting it as precisely as possible in its proper historical context. The corrective which is needed is a greater refinement in our understanding of the past, not wholesale abandonment of the project.

We can now see more clearly why Bultmann and others were so sceptical about the value of the contents of the gospels as evidence for the life and teaching of Jesus. Only part of the reason was the vicissitudes to which oral tradition is prone. They were also convinced that a true understanding of many pericopae led inevitably to the conclusion that they bore too many marks of a Hellenistic environment to have arisen in the Palestinian milieu in which Jesus moved. Thus many individual sayings were regarded as the creation of the later church to express its faith in the Risen Lord, and the similarity in form and conception between the miracle stories of Jesus and stories about pagan miracle workers were held to show that these stories were invented by the Hellenistic church to express their faith in Jesus in vivid terms. It has been precisely the expansion of our knowledge of Palestinian thought, made possible particularly by the discovery of the Dead Sea Scrolls, which has rendered many of Bultmann's conclusions questionable. This is not to say, however, that we can safely assume either that all the gospel traditions could have been formulated in a Palestinian environment or, even if they were, that all were equally authentic testimonies to what Jesus did and taught. We shall return to this question in chapter 9.

In this chapter we have attempted to illustrate the way form criticism works and to review some of the questions connected with it. There is no doubt that, largely because of the conclusions to which some of its exponents have come concerning the historical reliability of the gospels, the method has met with much criticism and resistance. Whatever conclusions we draw about history, however, there can be no going back on the contribution which the method has made to our understanding of the New Testament over the last fifty years, and this is increasingly recognized even in English-speaking countries, where some of the fiercest last-ditch battles against it have been fought.

7. Behind the Written Word – 2

The methods of form criticism can be applied, with modifications, to other parts of the New Testament.

An obvious candidate for an approach which has proved fruitful with the other gospels is the gospel of John, but it is made more difficult by the distinctive character of the book. This gospel presents many problems which have long baffled its interpreters. It is difficult to reach firm conclusions not only about its author but about those for whom it was written, the purpose it was intended to fulfil, and the particular movements of thought within the early church it represented. Even an exact analysis of its composition is difficult to achieve. In addition to the features noted in chapter 5 (*see* page 60) which distinguish this gospel from the other three, there are many inconsistencies both in narrative and in teaching. Examples of these are John 7:21-24 where the impression is given of continuing the conversation of chapter five, in spite of the intervention of chapter six; 14:31 which does not lead, as one might expect, to any departure from the house; and 5:24 which appears to conflict with 5:28f and 6:44.

There is no agreement among scholars at present on any of these points. On the one hand is the view of those who begin from the overwhelming impression the gospel gives, that it is the work of a distinctive personality with a highly individual style. To attempt to identify sources, or detect the hand of an editor or interpolator, is doomed to failure, as the many conflicting theories of redaction and rearrangement show. If sources were used, they have been for the most part too thoroughly assimilated for us to retrieve them. At most one might accept that the gospel was left unfinished by its author, and that in some passages it presents us with alternative drafts of the same material.

On the other hand are those who hold that a more precise analysis is possible. Some have held that the author used several quite extensive written sources which he roughly combined: for example, a 'book of signs' – beginning with the wedding at Cana (cf. 2:11) and the healing of the officer's son (cf. 4:46ff and 54), and concluding with 20:30f – combined with a collection of sayings and a passion narrative. Another approach has been to explain at least some of the inconsistencies by a theory of re-arrangement, on the assumption that (perhaps accidentally) the original order of the pages was disturbed. A third suggestion has been that the text was tampered with by a later editor with a different, perhaps more 'orthodox' point of view. Some scholars have employed all these approaches simultaneously in an attempt to account for all aspects of the problem.

Although form criticism is therefore much more difficult to apply to John's gospel, there is scope for its use. However much they have been written up, the miracle stories follow a similar outline to those in the synoptic gospels, as we saw with the feeding of the multitude, and while the long speeches of Jesus in John have no strict analogy in the other gospels, individual sayings nevertheless do sometimes show similarities of form, and in some cases of content as well. Compare John 13:20 – 'He who receives anyone I send receives me; he who receives me receives him who sent me' – with Matthew 10:40 – 'He who accepts you accepts me, and he who accepts me accepts him who commissioned me'. The vocabulary is different, but the basic ideas and the form of the saying are the same. Much still needs to be done in this area, but there is scope in John's gospel (within its special limitations) for the form critical method to bring out, as in the synoptic gospels, the characteristic features of material which was first passed on orally. Where this can be done, the role of the evangelist as conserver of traditional say-ings and stories, and not as innovator, is emphasized.

The same is true of other parts of the New Testament. We saw in the last chapter (page 73) that in I Corinthians 11:23 and 15:1 Paul refers to teaching he had given at Corinth, using the terms *received* and *handed on* which suggest oral tradition. In both cases Paul emphasizes that the teaching is not his own but something with which he has been entrusted, and this is borne out by the content of the verses which follow, for in both passages we have a recital of events connected with Jesus at which, with one exception, Paul was not himself present.

But Paul uses the terms *delivered, received* and *tradition* elsewhere. In Galatians 1:9 and I Thessalonians 2:13 he refers to the gospel as he had proclaimed it and his readers had received it, and in I Corinthians 11:2, I Thessalonians 4:1, Philippians 4:9 and elsewhere, he refers to the way of life appropriate to the Christian, which he had taught his converts. All this was tradition, handed on and received. Particularly important is Romans 6:17, in which Paul, writing to a church which he had not himself founded, appeals to the 'pattern of teaching' to which, as a guiding principle, the Roman Christians had been handed over. Traditional teaching was not therefore a peculiarity of Paul's missionary activity: he could assume its presence in churches he had never visited, and could be sure enough of its contents to base an appeal in his letters upon it.

By what means may we recover the contents of this tradition? I Corinthians 15:3ff provides some clues. It is clear that in passing on the tradition of Jesus' resurrection appearances Paul did not leave it entirely as he had received it; in verse 8 he has added his own name to the list of witnesses. Yet many of the characteristics of the passage suggest that substantially we have the tradition in the words in which it came to him. It has a rhythmic style (note the repetition of *that he* . . . and *according to the scriptures*); it contains Greek expressions not found elsewhere in Paul's writings (*appeared* and *according to the scriptures*); and it reads like a summary of the message of Jesus' death and resurrection. It certainly contains more information than Paul needed for his argument in the immediate context, which concerned only the resurrection. Style, vocabulary and content therefore confirm Paul's description of the passage as traditional teaching which he had received and passed on.

We have no formal quotations of traditional teaching explicitly introduced as such in Paul's letters apart from the two passages in I Corinthians, presumably because the need for them did not arise. But there may well be unheralded quotations and echoes elsewhere, and if we apply the criteria which are suggested by I Corinthians 15, we may recover some of them. An example often quoted is Romans 1:3-4, in which Paul summarizes the gospel. Stylistically the statements fall roughly into two corresponding halves:

born – Son of David – according to the flesh:
declared – Son of God – according to the Spirit;

this recalls the parallelism which was a regular feature of poetry in Hebrew and Aramaic. Of the vocabulary used, the verb translated *declared* in the New English Bible is unique in Paul, as is the particular expression here translated *Holy Spirit*. As to content, nowhere else does Paul make use of the idea that Jesus was the Son of David, or link Jesus' being Son of God with his resurrection. Thus, while there is no explicit statement that Paul is employing a quotation here, it seems likely that he took the opportunity – at the beginning of a letter to a church to which he was not personally known (at least, not to the majority) – to quote a traditional form of words which he had not himself composed, but whose meaning he could endorse and which he thought would be familiar to his readers, much as today a preacher might quote without acknowledgement well-known phrases from a hymn or collect because of the evocative power of the words for his hearers.

Detective work of this kind is of course much easier with the writings of Paul, because the quantity of material at our disposal makes it more easy to identify his customary ways of thinking and expressing himself. Even here we cannot expect mathematical precision, or universal agreement among experts. The conclusions must be tentative and open to amendment. There is quite wide agreement, for example, in regarding Philippians 2: 6-11 as a quotation of traditional material, much less concerning Colossians 1:15-20, and less still in determining the original form and meaning of either passage and the amendments, if any, which the author may have made when taking them over.

In some cases it is possible to extend this approach to other parts of the New Testament. A further clue which can often be followed in such cases is the occurrence of a particular phrase or set of ideas in several documents by different authors, where there is no other evidence to suggest literary borrowing. For example, in Colossians 3:8-4:1 there is a sequence in which first the readers are exhorted to lay aside all evil, and then, a few verses later, the reciprocal responsibilities of three different social groupings in the church are set out (wives and husbands, children and parents, slaves and masters) with emphasis upon being obedient to authority. It is not surprising that this sequence also occurs in Ephesians 4:25-31, 5:21-6:9, in view of the close links which, as we have already observed, exist between these two epistles; nor is it surprising that the idea of obedience to authority, with reference to the state, recurs in another Pauline letter, in Romans 13:1-7 and 12. But the same pattern is to be detected outside Paul, in I Peter 2:1, 2:13-3:8 and 5:1-5, and there are echoes of it also in James 1:21 and 4:7, and Hebrews 12:1 and 9. Readers should note especially, in comparing these passages, the recurrence of certain key words, *lay aside, away with, throw off* (all alternative renderings in the New English Bible of the same Greek word), and *be subject, be submissive, submit* (again only one Greek word is used). Some scholars have accordingly concluded that the authors of all these documents were making use of a common pattern of ethical teaching in a kind of early catechism, familiar to their readers, as a foundation upon which to build what they wished to say.

So far our review has assumed that the setting in which such traditional material was used (its *Sitz im Leben*) was teaching and preaching. It has been argued that a sharp distinction was drawn · in the church between these two activities, between *didache* (teaching) on the one hand and *kerygma* (preaching) on the other, the one being directed to converts and the other to outsiders. We need not doubt that there was some difference both in the subjects dealt with and in the manner of dealing with them, but the two terms are not always used in the New Testament in a precise, technical way to distinguish one from the other; and in any case the fact that we can recover samples of 'preaching' from letters which are essentially 'teaching' shows that a rigid separation between the two was not maintained. For evidence that there were standard ways of setting forth the message for fresh hearers and indicating the response to be made we may refer to Romans 10:8-9, which speaks of the 'word of faith which we proclaim', and goes on to mention believing and confessing Jesus as Lord in a way which recalls Acts 2:38 and 16:31. How far we can now recover the content of the preaching upon which the early church was founded (the *kerygma*) is open to debate. Certainly there are passages in Paul which suggest that for him the basic message included the coming of Christ, his death and resurrection according to the

88

Scriptures, his exaltation as the Lord and the expectation of his return in glory as judge. (See for example Romans 1:1-4, 2:16, 10:8f; I Corinthians 15:3f; Galatians 1:3f, 3:1; I Thessalonians 1:10.) These themes recur, with others, in some of the sermons in the early chapters of Acts (though surprisingly hardly at all in the two examples given of Paul's preaching to Gentiles in Acts 14:15-17 and 17:22-31). On the strength of this some scholars, particularly C. H. Dodd, have held that from the sermons in Acts the kerygma of the early church can be reconstructed in some detail. What is not so clear, however, is whether the pattern was universally followed in all areas, nor whether all the elements which appear in Acts were constant features of it. In any case, when we speak of the kerygma, we appear to be concerned with a common pattern of subjects to be dealt with, not a set form of words to be reproduced by the preacher on every occasion.

There were however other settings for traditional material beside teaching and public preaching. By means of it we are brought into touch with the confessions of faith and expressions of praise and prayer of the early church's worship. Examples can be seen in I Corinthians 8:6, and Ephesians 5:14, and longer passages in Philippians 2:6-11 and (probably) Colossians 1:15-20. Particularly notable in this connexion are the expressions which the Greek-speaking church retained in Aramaic, *Abba*, Father, (Romans 8:15, Galatians 4:6), *Marana tha*, Our Lord, come, (I Corinthians 16:22), *Amen* (Romans 11:36, etc.), presumably because already, before the gospel had begun to be preached in Greek-speaking areas, these words had established themselves in the language of worship, and had resisted translation.

A further range of common material which seems to have been employed in many settings, including controversy, and perhaps simply study for its own sake, is derived from the Old Testament. The New Testament is permeated at every level by the Old. The faith and religious practices of Israel are the starting point and presupposition, even where Christian writers proceed to distinguish their beliefs from them. In fundamental assumptions about God, and in the use of religious vocabulary and imagery, the influence of the Old Testament is to be found on every page. Beyond this however there is the deliberate use of

Old Testament quotations to undergird argument, as in Romans 3:1-20 and throughout the letter to the Hebrews; as a basis for exhortation and warning, as in I Corinthians 10:1-13; to illuminate events in the story of Jesus by showing them to be the fulfilment of prophecy, as in John 19:24; and in other ways. Often a formula is used to introduce the quotation (*as it is written . . .,* etc.); in other cases, as in Mark 14:62, the source of the words quoted is not acknowledged, but the fact that they are derived from the Old Testament is nevertheless fundamental to what is being said. At the present time the use of the Old Testament in the New is the subject of intensive study, and the problems involved are complex. Often the quotation does not coincide precisely with the text of the Old Testament in the Hebrew or any of the Greek versions known to us, and it is not certain whether the Old Testament text has been adapted to its Christian purpose or whether a variant text, now lost, is being cited. Occasionally, as in Jude 6 and 9, there are quotations from and allusions to books which were not included in the Old Testament when the Canon was finally fixed. In a few cases the source of a quotation introduced as scripture is not known to us at all (*see* James 4:5).

A special feature of the use of the Old Testament is the way in which the same text is used by different New Testament writers in different ways (e.g. Genesis 15:6 in Romans 4:3, Galatians 3:6 and James 2:23; or Habakkuk 2:4 in Romans 1:17, Galatians 3:11 and Hebrews 10:38). Sometimes too texts from different places in the Old Testament are combined. An important example of this is the passages relating to the 'stone' (Isaiah 8:14, 28:16) which are quoted in combination, but for different purposes, both in Romans 9:32-3 and (with Psalm 118:22 which is itself quoted elsewhere) in I Peter 2:6-8. Whether the explanation for all this is that there existed in the early church a 'book of testimonies' or a selection of Old Testament excerpts suitable for Christian purposes, as some have argued, or that the use of the Old Testament was governed only by custom in oral teaching, it is clear that certain Old Testament passages were influential in Christian thinking before they were used by any of our New Testament writers. In fact what emerges very clearly from the study of the Old Testament in the New is that Old Testament interpretation figured very prominently in the life of the church. The Jewish Scriptures, and in particular parts of the prophets and the psalms, were closely studied with the special intention of discovering clues for understanding the death and resurrection of Jesus. Some of the interpretations strike the modern reader as somewhat forced, although this impression would not necessarily have been given in the setting of Jewish biblical interpretation at the time. The interpretation of the Old Testament was a key factor in the development of New Testament teaching, and illustrates the point made in chapter 3 that in the earliest period the Old Testament provided the Scriptures of the church.

The advantages of the approach to the New Testament we have been describing are obvious. First, as we saw when we first met form criticism in connexion with the synoptic gospels, it helps to supplement our knowledge of the history of the early church. This additional help is much needed, because we really know very little about the history of the church in its earliest period. The book of Acts is the only work we possess explicitly dealing with it, and even a cursory glance at its contents shows that it leaves much to be desired as a historical record. In the first half it concentrates much of the time on Peter, and in the second half is concerned only with Paul. Comparison with his letters shows that much of Paul's career has been omitted, and at certain points it is difficult to reconcile what Acts tells us about him with the information provided by his letters.

The historical worth of Acts is disputed. Some scholars accept its narrative as a substantially accurate account of events. On the one hand they argue that Luke is likely to have been just as faithful to his sources in writing Acts as he was to Mark in writing his gospel; on the other hand they are able to cite evidence from inscriptions and other archaeological discoveries which show that Luke was meticulously accurate in reproducing local details about the towns Paul visited on his journeys. Others, however, do not find these arguments persuasive. They differentiate between the kind of background detail and local colour that any conscientious writer might have been able to acquire by research, and the reconstruction of the course of events in the life of the early church, for which Luke may not have had any sources comparable to those he used for the gospel. While the early church obviously had a strong motive for preserving traditions about Jesus, what motive would there have been for preserving traditions about the details of its own history? Thus they argue that while Luke doubtless did his best with the material available, and Acts may contain much important historical information, we should not discount the effect of Luke's own idealism and possible misunderstanding in his reconstruction of the course of events. This is so even if we assume what is by no means certain, that Luke merely wished to narrate 'what had happened', without offering any interpretation or advocating a point of view for the benefit of the contemporary church. Indeed, some would wish to emphasize the theological purpose of Acts as more fundamental than any desire to write history.

In particular this debate concerns the early sermons in Acts. Those who, like C. H. Dodd, regard them as evidence for the earliest Christian preaching, treat them, if not as verbatim reports of what was actually said on each occasion, at least as fair representations, based on early traditional material. Others hold that they are Luke's own imaginative reconstructions, representing his view of what must have been said, written in an appropriate style, and intended like the speeches inserted into their narratives by other ancient historians as a commentary upon the course of events. At present it can only be said that the debate between these two points of view continues, with perhaps growing emphasis on the second.

On any view of Acts, however, we need all the supplementary information about the early history of the church that we can obtain. Some additional information can be derived from the New Testament letters, especially Paul's, and from Revelation wherever events and personalities are mentioned. But for the ideas and everyday practices of the church, the work done on the traditions behind the writings is invaluable.

The second advantage of this approach is that research into these traditions sets the writers of the New Testament in their proper context in the life of the church. Each writer of course has his own contribution to make, but it is a mistake to think of them too much in isolation. If we do so, the similarities between them, whether in ideas or in actual language, become explicable only in terms of literary dependence: one writer, we will have to assume, has read and borrowed material from another. Sometimes this is clearly the correct solution. II Peter and Jude and the synoptic gospels can be accounted for only in this way. But this should be limited to cases where the parallels between documents are extensive and close, and include distinctive expressions which are unlikely to have been commonplace in oral tradition.

This has particular application to St. Paul. It has been fashionable at certain periods to emphasize the difference between the teaching of Jesus in the synoptic gospels and the teaching of Paul, to the point of claiming that Paul rather than Jesus was the founder of Christianity as we now know it, with the implication that it would have been better for the world if the simpler teaching of Jesus, free of supposedly Pauline distortions, had held the field. We shall return later to the question of the assumptions about the teaching of Jesus which this view implied, but for the moment we can note that the discovery of traditional elements in the teaching of Paul has made it clear that he was by no means the complete innovator in Christian doctrine he was once thought to be.

Indeed it emerges more clearly than ever that behind the writings of the New Testament, diverse as they are in many respects, there lies a unity in the life and thought of the early church. We should not idealize that unity, as though there were no conflicts or contradictions (Paul's letters make it abundantly plain that there were many), yet there were common factors which justify speaking of one Christian movement rather than a series of separate movements, not the least of these being the use of the Old Testament, the conviction that belief in God had its focal point in Jesus Christ, and a similar life-style for which the key word was *love*.

Thirdly, research into the traditions on which they depended actually brings the originality of the New Testament writers into sharper relief. Although the writers used traditional material, they remain authors in their own right, and the more precisely we are able to identify the teaching of the church with which they were familiar, the more clearly we can see not only how each writer is indebted to the church, but what precisely his distinctive contribution was. Paul again is the obvious example. His work bears vividly the marks of his rugged and explosive personality and the quality of his intellect. Whatever he owed theologically to the church which he had once persecuted, the conflicts in which his letters show him engaged prove that he was by no means merely repeating conventional doctrines. While his missionary journeys were themselves an important factor in carrying the Christian faith to the Gentile world, his more fundamental contribution was to spell out the terms of admission of Gentiles to the church. Without the theological battles which he fought in order to do this it is doubtful whether Christianity would ever have spread in the way it did. What was at stake was whether the church should be considered as a sect within Judaism, incapable of existing on its own, or rather as the fulfilment of Judaism, standing in its own right and open to all races. But Paul is not the only creative figure whom we meet in the New Testament. The authors of Hebrews, of John's gospel, of Revelation, or of the smaller epistles, are all individuals, and part of the excitement of studying their work is the discovery that we are encountering living people through what they have written. It cannot be stressed too often that behind the pages of the New Testament there stand the Christian men and women who shared in producing it.

8. Collectors or Editors?

We ended the last chapter by pointing out that the study of the underlying traditions in the New Testament by means of form criticism highlights the individuality of its various authors. We now return to the synoptic gospels to consider the implications of this.

To some extent all four evangelists have for long been thought of as individuals, and the traditional symbols with which they have been associated in the history of Christian art, the man, the lion, the ox and the eagle, were attempts to express some of the characteristics of each gospel in terms of the four living creatures of Revelation 4:7. But since the development of synoptic studies with the tendency to see two evangelists as taking over and editing the work of the third and to think of all three as reproducing material from oral tradition, it has not been easy to think of the authors as having any creative role in the composition of their work. Until twenty-five years ago there were few serious studies of the theology of Matthew, Mark, or Luke, in contrast to the many works on the theology of John. Now, however, attention has turned from the traditions behind the gospels to the way in which the authors have used them. Scholars have begun to ask what purposes the evangelists had in mind, and for the answer they have looked particularly at the apparently trivial alterations which the evangelists made to their sources. To understand the gospels fully we must go beyond the study of the traditions they contain and consider the evangelists' redaction, or editing of them.

Each of the synoptic gospels contains an account of the baptism of Jesus, differing in details and in the context in which it is set. By careful comparison we shall try to pinpoint the precise differences and assess their implications. To do this it is essential to put to one side the questions usually asked, about what actually happened and what the baptism meant to Jesus, and concentrate rather on how each evangelist presents the baptism and uses it in his gospel. This is not easy, because unlike the first readers we are familiar with all three gospels, and in reading one version we easily assume details mentioned only in another.

We will begin, as Matthew and Luke did, with Mark. Mark opens his gospel, 'Here begins the gospel of Jesus Christ' (1:1), and turns immediately to a composite quotation from Malachi 3:1, Exodus 23:20 and Isaiah 40:3, which points to the coming of two figures from God, one in preparation for the other (verses 2f). There follows a brief description of John the Baptist, his preaching in the wilderness, the crowds who came to him, his dress and diet. One quotation of his preaching is given, his announcement of the Stronger One following him, who would baptize with the Holy Spirit (verses 4-8). We then move straight on to Jesus coming from Nazareth, his baptism, the descent of the Spirit and the voice from heaven, 'Thou art my Son, my Beloved; on thee my favour rests' (verses 9-11). (The alternative version given in the margin of Mark and Matthew in the New English Bible is a matter of translation only, not of different manuscript readings.)

We do not need to go into all the details of this passage to see the general effect. In no more than eleven verses we are presented with a triple testimony to the significance of Jesus: Scripture, the Baptist and the voice of God. The Old Testament prophecy, we are told, is now fulfilled. That fact in itself is significant, for prophecy as the early church understood it concerned not a number of unrelated and trivial future events, but a series of connected happenings which make up *the* event, God's intervention in judgement and salvation to fulfil his purposes for the world and for his people. So, Mark is saying, the Day has now come, the age of fulfilment has dawned. That is how both John and Jesus are to be understood.

John in this setting fulfils two functions. On the one hand he is part of the evidence that the prophecy has reached fulfilment. That is why his ministry in the desert is mentioned. On the other hand his role is that of the forerunner. Simply by his presence, but also by his message, he points forward to Jesus who is stronger and greater and will baptize with the Spirit. It is remarkable how little else we are told about John. Even the brief note about his clothing and food in verse 6 is intended to

96

stress the fulfilment of prophecy. The clothing is that of the prophet Elijah in II Kings 1:8. In Malachi the messenger who will prepare the way of the Lord is identified as Elijah (cf. Malachi 3:1 with 4:5). So, Mark emphasizes, all aspects of the prophecy have been fulfilled, a point confirmed in Mark 9:13. The forerunner has come, as Scripture declared he would.

So Jesus, in fulfilment of both scriptural and contemporary promise, comes to Jordan and is baptized. He sees the heavens split open and the Spirit descending, and hears the voice of God (verses 10f). The coming of the Spirit is a further sign that the age of salvation has dawned, as well as marking Jesus out from other men. We do not need to decide here whether the words from heaven recall both Psalm 2:7 and Isaiah 42:1, as most commentators agree, or only the Isaiah passage. What stands out clearly is that Jesus is authoritatively acknowledged to be the Son of God, a title which is given prominence in Mark's gospel, from the opening verse (if the reading of the majority of manuscripts is genuine), through the cries of defeated evil spirits (3:11, 5:7), to the confession of the centurion at the cross (15:39). As Mark describes the baptismal scene, the descent of the Spirit and the heavenly voice are vouchsafed to Jesus alone; they are not public events. In the gospel generally Jesus tries to keep the secret of his true nature concealed from the public until the end. It is for the sake of his readers that Mark narrates these events. We are to know who Jesus is, and that his ministry as Son of God has now begun.

Immediately Jesus is driven into the wilderness by the Spirit to be tempted (verses 12f). Nothing is said of fasting or prayer; only that he was in the company of wild beasts and that angels attended him, with the implication that the temptations were resisted and the tempter defeated. Although the language is terse and allusive, it may well be that we are to see here a contrast with the fall of Adam whom the angels drove out from the garden of God. The reversal of man's defeat by evil has begun. Thereafter the public ministry in Galilee gets under way.

By means of this introduction we are to understand the rest of the gospel. Through the triple attestation by Scripture, the Baptist and the heavenly voice, the reader can recognize Jesus

97

as the fulfiller of prophecy, the inaugurator of the new age, God's Son, and the adversary of Satan, even though his journey will take him through rejection to the cross.

In neither Matthew nor Luke does the baptism have the same introductory function. Matthew begins with a genealogy of Jesus (1:1-17), Luke with the birth of John (1:5-25, 57-80), and both continue with narratives of Jesus' birth (Matthew 1:18–2:23; Luke 1:26-56; 2:1-52). In both gospels therefore the scene is set in other ways before we come to the Baptist's ministry. The emphasis has shifted in other respects too:

(a) Both Matthew and Luke have included, along with details taken from Mark, 'Q' material about John's preaching, which spells out the summons to repentance (Matthew 3:7-10, Luke 3: 7-9). This means that the interest of John for these two evangelists is not only in his prophecy concerning Jesus but also more generally in his preaching. In this way both gospels bring out more clearly that repentance is a necessary preparation for the coming of Jesus. Luke adds to this a short section (3:10-14) which sets out by a series of questions and answers those 'fruits of repentance' for which John has called. A further effect of this additional material is that John's preaching in both Matthew and Luke stresses that the coming one will come as judge. This gives added point to the saying, which Mark has but does not develop, that John is unworthy of Jesus (Mark 1:7).

(b) The two later gospels also include 'Q' material about the temptations, so that instead of a bare report of the temptation of Jesus and his victory, we are now given an account of the nature of the temptations and the way in which the victory was won (Matthew 4:1-11, Luke 4:1-13). In both accounts, the divine announcement *Thou art my Son* is taken up by the tempter in the words *If you are the Son of God* and Jesus by his replies proves its truth.

Turning now to Matthew, we notice that in the narrative of the actual baptism Matthew follows Mark quite closely, but inserts two verses which continue the theme of John's unworthiness (Matthew 3:14-15). John is unwilling to baptize Jesus; rather he should himself be baptized by him. This insertion is significant. The more Jesus' role as the righteous judge is emphasized, as it is in Matthew, the more it is likely that his submission to John for baptism will become a theological problem.

98

Later writers also had to wrestle with this. Jesus' reply is equally significant: 'Let it be so for the present; we do well to conform in this way to all that God requires,' or more literally, 'thus it is fitting for us to fulfil all righteousness'. The words *fulfil* and *righteousness* are characteristic of this gospel. The former occurs sixteen times as compared with three in Mark and nine in Luke. According to 5:17, Jesus has come not to abolish the law but to fulfil it, and Matthew is punctuated throughout by Old Testament prophecies which are said to be fulfilled in Jesus. *Righteousness* occurs once only in Luke, never in Mark, but seven times in Matthew, and the adjective *righteous* eleven times in Luke, two in Mark, seventeen in Matthew. In the Sermon on the Mount the disciples are to seek first God's kingdom and his righteousness (6:33); their righteousness must exceed the scribes' and Pharisees' (5:20); they are to hunger and thirst after it (5:6). The righteousness of Jesus himself is acknowledged by Judas, Pilate and Pilate's wife (27:4, 19, 24, but texts vary). The words of Jesus at his baptism are therefore deeply connected with the presentation of Jesus and his message in the gospel as a whole. At his baptism Jesus humbles himself, being baptized by John as sinners were, although as the righteous one he has, unlike them, no sins to confess. But this does not cast doubt upon his righteousness; rather it confirms it. It is in his ministry for others that Jesus fulfils the righteousness God requires of men. With that reply added point is given to the words from heaven (adapted from Mark), 'This is my beloved Son, on whom my favour rests'. We notice the subtle change which (according to most manuscripts) Matthew has made in them: no longer are they spoken to Jesus, as God's assurance to him which the reader overhears; they are now spoken about Jesus to John (perhaps to bystanders too), in reassurance confirming Jesus' reply to John's objection. God acknowledges Jesus as his righteous son. It is also worth observing, in view of what we shall find in Luke, that in Matthew John is closely associated with Jesus' fulfilment of righteousness. Just as in this gospel John anticipates Jesus' message, proclaiming like Jesus the nearness of the kingdom (cf. 3:2 with 4:17, a similarity found only in Matthew), so John's ministry is essential to that of Jesus (*'we* do well to conform . . .' 3:15). Although one is unworthy of the other, they are collaborators as the kingdom comes.

Thus, by giving the baptism a new setting, by introducing new material containing ideas strongly characteristic of his gospel as a whole, and by changing slightly what he has taken over from Mark, Matthew has brought quite new emphases to the story.

This is also true of Luke in a different way. In general as we have seen, Luke, like Matthew, has expanded the context of the baptism. We shall not consider here the question of the (probably incorrect) alternative reading in Luke 3:22, which would make the words from heaven a straight quotation of Psalm 2:7, but two important differences must be discussed:

(1) Before the baptism of Jesus Luke inserts a brief description of the arrest and imprisonment of John (3:19f). At first sight this might be regarded simply as an attempt to tidy up Mark's narrative. Mark has a brief reference to John's arrest at a slightly later point, after Jesus' baptism and before he begins his preaching (1:14), and an extended account of the reasons for the arrest and John's eventual murder, in the style of a 'flash-back', in 6:14-29. Luke, however, in his parallel to Mark 6:16 in 9:9, simply has Herod recalling the murder. The arrest he describes before Jesus is baptized in 3:19f, the murder itself he does not describe at all. The problem of when to describe events which run parallel to the main story is one which authors often have to face. But the effect of Luke's rearrangement is to create two separate sections, one dealing with John's ministry and the other with that of Jesus, and to give the impression that the baptism of Jesus did not occur until after John's arrest. In the description of the baptism (Luke 3:21f) John's name is not mentioned at all; the verb used is in the passive. We often miss the implication of this because, even when we read Luke we have in mind Mark's different order of events, but two other passages suggest that the impression Luke creates was deliberate. (a) Luke 16:16 draws a distinction between the period of time during which the law and the prophets were operative, and the subsequent time when the kingdom is preached. John appears to belong to the former period, as can be seen by contrasting the saying with the parallel version in Matthew 11:12-13. Here a similar distinction is drawn between the two periods of time but John is included in the period of the kingdom (a version which corresponds to the role of John in Matthew 3). Whether the difference between the two

sayings is due to Luke's editing or to his use of a different version from Matthew's, the effect in Luke is to draw a line of demarcation between Jesus and John. (b) In Acts 10:37-8, in a summary of the gospel in Peter's sermon to Cornelius, we find a similar distinction. Jesus begins his ministry *after* John's preaching of baptism. Again nothing is said about John baptizing him; on the contrary it is God who anoints him with his Holy Spirit and power. It would therefore seem that Luke was deliberately trying to create the impression, contrary to Mark, that John's ministry had come to an end before the ministry of Jesus began. (2) In contrast to Mark, Luke reduces the reference to the actual baptism in 3:21f to a bare minimum, and lays all the stress upon the coming of the Spirit and the voice from heaven. The New English Bible well reproduces here the force of the original Greek, which by the structure of the sentence throws all the weight upon what comes at the end, and treats the first part, including the baptism, as merely setting the scene for it. The significance of the baptism is still further reduced by the fact that Luke inserts a reference to Jesus praying. This is a typically Lukan touch; he often represents Jesus as a man of prayer. But the effect in this passage is to put the baptism on a level with it. It is difficult to escape the conclusion that Luke is deliberately minimizing the importance of Jesus' baptism in water. He cannot eliminate it altogether, for it is too firmly embedded in Christian tradition, but he puts the emphasis on other elements in the story.

The reason for both these changes is probably to be found in Luke's understanding of the ministry of Jesus. It is often pointed out that Luke is interested in the Holy Spirit; this applies not only to the Spirit's work in relation to believers but to Jesus as well. So in Acts 10:38 God is said to have anointed him with the Holy Spirit and with power. The verb *anointed* used here is significant: for as the noun *Messiah* means *anointed one*, so the verb *anoint* can mean *induct into office as the Messiah*. Jesus' messianic ministry is performed in the power of the Spirit. In Luke 4:16-21 Jesus begins his sermon in Nazareth by quoting Isaiah 61:1, 'The Spirit of the Lord is upon me', and in 4:1 Luke modifies Mark's description of the Spirit driving Jesus into the wilderness so as to read, 'And Jesus, *full of the Holy Spirit*, returned from the Jordan and was led by the Spirit in the desert'.

It is in keeping with this that in 3:21f the real beginning of Jesus' ministry should be marked not by his baptism in water but by his endowment with the Spirit, and that for the same reason John should be removed from effective participation in the scene. Several times in his writings Luke uses various versions of a saying contrasting John's baptism with that of Jesus. While they end differently, all begin with the same point: John's baptism is baptism in water only. Luke wants to leave no ambiguity here. Jesus' ministry is authorized not by man but by God, not with water but with the Spirit.

Two other distinctive features of Luke may be briefly mentioned. We have noted that Mark represents the opening of the heavens and the descent of the Spirit as visible only to Jesus (*he saw*, 1:10). Matthew makes the heavenly voice audible to John, but in the main he follows Mark. In Luke however they are real events in the external world. The phrase *he saw* is omitted, and the words *in bodily form* are added to the description of the Spirit as a dove (3:21f). There is no possibility in Luke of interpreting these events merely as a subjective vision experienced by Jesus. We observe the same stress on external reality in the story of the resurrection appearance in Jerusalem (Luke 24:36-43), perhaps for the same reason: there were those who were inclined to dismiss these things as only 'in the mind', and Luke was contradicting them.

It is also interesting that Luke has inserted between the baptism and temptations his version of the genealogy of Jesus (3:23-38). This has often caused perplexity. Some have seen in it support for the 'Proto-Luke' theory, arguing that originally the gospel began in chapter 3, where the genealogy would have occupied a position more similar to that in Matthew, but before we resort to theories of this kind we should pay more attention to what the genealogy contains. It is often pointed out that, while Matthew traces Jesus' genealogy back to Abraham, Luke traces it to Adam, thereby universalizing the significance of Jesus. While this is true, it must also be noted that Adam is not the last in the series of fathers and sons. He in turn is the son of God (3:38). Coming between the declaration 'Thou art my Son' and the temptations, which in their 'Q' form test Jesus on this very point, the position of Luke's genealogy is very significant. The first Adam was son of God, but fell to Satan.

Jesus, the second Adam, is also Son of God, but overcomes the tempter.

Whether or not all the suggestions made in the above interpretation of the baptism narratives are correct, the discussion illustrates the approach of redaction criticism and the methods it employs. Redaction criticism builds upon form criticism and the older source analysis of the gospels. It is assumed that Matthew and Luke used Mark, and that the material available to them was in the form of separate pericopae. (If the opponents of Streeter's theory of the priority of Mark should at any time prove their case, all the work done by redaction critics so far would have to be done again from a different starting point.) Attention is given especially to parallel passages where the peculiar features of each gospel can be pin-pointed. Omissions and additions, rearrangements of order, and the occurrence of words and subjects distinctive of a gospel (or in the case of Luke, of the gospel and Acts together) are weighed carefully to see what they will yield in the way of clues to the author's purpose. Of particular interest, where they occur, are the editorial phrases or extended summary passages which link pericopae together; they are the evangelist's own cement with which he holds together the component parts of the gospel he is constructing. The aim is to recover, it has been said, the third *Sitz im Leben* of the gospel material, the first 'setting-in-life' being (in some cases at least) the setting of a saying or occurrence in the life of Jesus, the second the setting of that tradition as transmitted orally in the life of the church, and the third its use by the evangelist, in the composition of his gospel.

The conviction from which all the redaction critics start, and which they believe their work has demonstrated, is that the purposes of the evangelists were primarily theological; they were not simply preservers of traditions which they feared would be lost to posterity if they did not write them down, nor were they mere chroniclers recording events; they were Christian teachers and preachers intending to set forth an understanding of Jesus and his gospel for the benefit of the church of their own day. Thus, in the narratives of the baptism of Jesus, the differences between the evangelists are due to their differing theological emphases, not simply to differences of opinion about what actually happened. This is a much more positive estimate of the role of the evangelist. It places the writers of the synoptic gospels on the same level (in purpose, if not in method and achievement) as the author of the gospel of John, and adds their names to the roll of constructive theologians of New Testament times.

It also offers a more satisfying answer to the question why we have four gospels. From as early as the second century when Tatian produced his famous *Diatessaron*, in which the four gospels were combined in a single narrative, people have asked this question. If the aim of the gospel writers were simply to record events, the differences between them would be hard to account for. Matthew and Luke might have added to Mark, but hardly altered, still less omitted anything of his. If however the evangelists had a different purpose, if each had something distinctive to say about Jesus, the existence of different gospels is explained, and the survival of all of them is justified.

At this stage, when the basic work is still being done, we should not expect unanimity as to what those purposes were, but many scholars would agree in general terms that Mark was writing for a church threatened with persecution, which needed to be reminded that Jesus is the Son of God because he was crucified, and that to follow him means to take up the cross; Matthew was providing a handbook of teaching for the leaders of a church in a Jewish environment which was in danger of losing its distinctiveness and becoming both slack and censorious; while Luke, writing for Gentile Christians of the second generation, set out in his two volumes, the gospel and the Acts, both a statement of what the gospel is and a demonstration of its universality.

There is a further advantage in the redaction-critical approach. It gives us good ground once more for studying the gospels in their entirety. At one time there was a tendency to treat them merely as quarries for material in reconstructing a historical account of Jesus of Nazareth. For this purpose John's gospel was more or less ignored; in the synoptics the tendency was to take what was presumed to be the most primitive version of each item as the most authoritative, and discount the rest. In practice this meant Mark's narrative, and those sayings from each gospel most easily restored to Aramaic. The usable portions of the gospels thus tended to be limited to what was considered historically reliable. Whatever may be the justification of this procedure in seeking historical information about Jesus, it does violence to the gospels as gospels. Each was produced to be read in its own right (or rather, heard in its own right, for in days of widespread illiteracy they were primarily read aloud). Redaction criticism seeks to do this: it treats the evangelists seriously as authors who intended to say what they said, without passing prior judgement on its value.

Thus redaction criticism is to be welcomed. It is a fruitful approach which is being widely explored, and modern commentaries are beginning to incorporate its insights. On the other hand, although it was first used a quarter of a century ago, even earlier if one takes one or two pioneers into account, there are still certain questions about its procedures which have not yet been fully resolved, and we must end this chapter by considering them.

The first concerns the danger of subjectivity. How do we determine what was in an author's mind? Apart from the general danger of reading into the words more than the writer intended by them, there is the problem which arises precisely because a gospel contains traditional material. For example, Matthew ends with a commission of the risen Jesus to the disciples to go and make disciples of all nations (28:19), but includes in 10:5f one of the most restrictive sayings in all the gospels, 'Do not take the road to gentile lands . . . but go rather to the lost sheep of the house of Israel'. Is there some elusive key which will help to reconcile these apparently contradictory statements, or should we take the view that only one of them represents the author's own view, the other being included, although he was aware of the contradiction, because it was part of the tradition of the sayings of Jesus which was handed down to him? In other words, how do we prove or disprove a theory about the teaching of a gospel? Is evidence which does not fit our theory to be dismissed as traditional material which the evangelist has not assimilated to his views, or is it decisive proof that the theory is wrong?

Redaction criticism is especially vulnerable to the charge of subjectivity when it is applied to the gospel of Mark. It must always be remembered that the only source of the synoptic gospels about which we can make even relatively confident assertions is Mark, as a source of Matthew and Luke. While we may infer the existence of other sources, we do not possess them and cannot with certainty reconstruct them. When we turn to Mark itself, how are we to distinguish the author's own contributions to his gospel from emphases which may have been present in the traditions he used? It is easy to fall into a circular argument, arbitrarily specifying Markan additions in order to lay bare the tradition he inherited, so as to show in turn what he has added to it!

The only safeguard against these dangers is to make disciplined use of objective data, of facts which are not themselves in dispute, even though they may be capable of more than one interpretation. It is not enough simply to form a subjective impression of the emphases and concerns of a gospel. Detailed analyses and comparisons are essential. The vocabulary and linguistic usage peculiar to each gospel must be accurately established, as a sign of the evangelist's own hand. Special attention must be given to those points in a gospel where the evangelist is most likely to have had to use his own initiative, namely in the editorial links between pericopae, which he is unlikely to have derived from tradition. Such data are available, but in consequence one of the potentially most illuminating and promising approaches to the gospels, from the point of view of the ordinary reader, tends in practice to be the most technical, and for the ordinary reader, unreadable. Only by dealing with minutiæ can sure results be obtained and subjectivity avoided.

The second question about redaction criticism concerns the degree of freedom which, it is claimed, the gospel writers exercised in their work. We have suggested above that Matthew and Luke deliberately introduced modifications into Mark's narrative in order to bring out emphases which they wished to make. But in comparing the gospels overall we may perhaps be more impressed by the later writers' fidelity to Mark. Clearly they could have introduced more extensive changes than they have. How far then have Matthew and Luke altered Mark freely rather than out of deference to alternative traditions? To be specific, is the little dialogue between Jesus and the Baptist concerning John's fitness to baptize Jesus a free creation by Matthew to answer a theological problem created by his own portrayal of the righteousness of Jesus, or is it on the contrary a tradition about the baptism of Jesus known to Matthew but not to Mark or Luke, with perhaps even a claim to being historical? It is not easy to answer this question. Clearly the possibility that Matthew and Luke have introduced alternative traditions in preference to Mark cannot be ruled out, but it is impossible to account for all their modifications in this way; they are too widespread. We should have to assume that everything Matthew took from Mark was also available to him in an alternative form which he preferred at various points, although often only for small details of wording. Such an hypothesis of two virtually identical sources is difficult to believe. In some cases, as in Matthew 3:14f, we are helped by the presence of words and ideas which are peculiar to the gospel concerned and are therefore likely to be due to its author.

It is possible to meet this difficulty, however, by observing that even if all the modifications introduced by an evangelist were due to tradition, we should still have to ask why he had preferred one version to another. Some insertions may have been made simply because the material was available, omissions simply because of pressure on space (a book written on a continuous roll could not be infinitely long) and changes because of alternative tradition; but in each case the evangelist evaluated the material according to some criterion, whether his own preference or the need of his readers. A study of the differences can still point us to the purposes of the evangelist.

We are of course assuming that the theological perspective or tendency of a gospel reflects the thought of its author. Some scholars have taken the view that this editorial work was more corporate than individual. There may have been a number of authors, working whether as a group of collaborators or in succession to each other, over a period of time, so that the finished product may reflect the mind of the Christian community rather than an individual. This has been suggested particularly in the case of Matthew. It is less easy to advocate for Luke, who uses the first person singular in his dedications (Luke 1:3; Acts 1:1). The advantage of this view is that it enables us to deal with inner contradictions in a gospel in terms of different stages of editing. On the other hand in such a case the distinction between tradition and redaction really breaks down, for the gospel would then contain a succession of redactions, and the

107

only distinguishing feature of the final one would be, not that it was designed to prepare the gospel for publication, but simply that no further redactions happened to follow it.

A further question concerning redaction criticism is more fundamental: is it true that the gospels are primarily theological documents? There were other ways of writing theology, as the rest of the New Testament illustrates. What led the evangelists to cast their theology in the form of narrative? The assumption widespread earlier in this and in all preceding centuries, at least as far as the synoptics are concerned, was that the gospels were primarily intended to record historical fact. Is the contention of the redaction critic that the gospels are primarily theological any more than an assumption from which he starts?

The test case for this question is Mark's outline of the ministry of Jesus, which Matthew and Luke follow in the main. Is this outline – beginning with Jesus' baptism and temptations and continuing through the Galilean ministry, the withdrawal to Caesarea Philippi, Peter's confession and the transfiguration, to the journey to Jerusalem and final ministry in the city – is this outline a scheme based on historical memory of the sequence of events in Jesus' life (that is, upon tradition)? Or is it an arrangement which Mark created, because it served his theological purposes better to deal first with the significance of Jesus' ministry to those 'outside', then to deal with the meaning of discipleship, confessing Jesus and following him to the cross, and finally with the basis of the confrontation with Judaism which led to the crucifixion? The fact that John's gospel offers a different arrangement underlines the dilemma. If both gospels are intended to be historical, one must be erroneous where they conflict. If one is based on a theological scheme, why not the other?

The answer to such questions must depend, at least to some extent, on whether a convincing theological analysis can be offered for each gospel. We have tried to show that the gospels do provide evidence of theological interests. But deeper issues are involved. Even if theological motives dictated the writing of the gospels, did the writers have no concern for history? What was their attitude to historical facts if they felt free to 'bend' them to suit theological ideas? Further, if we allow that they did this, how do we today go behind their 'distortions' to what actually

108

happened? These questions have arisen in connexion with redaction criticism, but they are equally relevant to form criticism. What historical reliability do the accounts of Jesus in our gospels have? To these questions, often raised and so far deferred in this book, we now turn.

9. The Jesus of History?

For many people the four gospels are the heart of the New Testament, bringing them into close contact with Jesus. They regard them as a direct transcript of his teaching and a precise account of what happened to him. This has been for centuries the accepted view. Although it was recognized in early times that there was a difference of style between John's gospel and the rest (see above, page 61), there was no serious doubt that in all four was to be found the historical truth about Jesus. The custom in some churches of standing for the gospel reading at the Eucharist is one evidence of this estimate: we encounter Jesus more directly in the gospels than in any other part of Scripture.

Today however this can no longer be taken for granted. While there are still scholars who take substantially the traditional view, they are now required to be on the defensive, and a wide variety of other positions are held. Most would hesitate to regard everything in the gospels as historically accurate, and some would ascribe most of their contents to the inventiveness of the church, acting under the compulsion of faith in the risen Lord rather than of historical fact.

There is no need to repeat from previous chapters the facts about the gospels which form the basis for these conclusions. We have seen evidence that the gospels are not the straightforward reminiscences of the eye-witness apostles, Matthew and John, nor of the apostles' associates, Mark and Luke, but collections of oral traditions which underwent considerable modification, both in the process of being handed on and when they were reduced to writing. Theological considerations influenced the process quite as much as, if not more than a concern for historical record. All three main elements in the gospels, the narrative framework, the individual narrative episodes (miracle stories, pronouncement stories, stories about Christ) and the individual sayings and complexes of sayings, have been subject to the formative hand of the church, although the precise extent of this is not agreed. This means that even those scholars who are most inclined to trust the gospels as essentially historical cannot put forward an assured picture of Jesus which will compel assent. Everything in the gospels is on trial.

Three factors especially encourage caution in estimating the historical worth of the gospel traditions. They are: (a) the anonymity of the tradition; (b) the role of Christian prophecy; and (c) the influence of the Old Testament.

(a) The New Testament epistles contain in various places echoes of the teaching of Jesus (cf. Romans 12:14 with Matthew 5:44 and Luke 6:28, or James 5:12 with Matthew 5:34-7), but only rarely is the source of the saying acknowledged. On only four occasions outside the gospels are sayings explicitly quoted as sayings of the Lord (I Corinthians 7:10f., 9:14; Acts 20:35, and possibly I Thessalonians 4:15f.), and of these there is no gospel version at all of the last two, and only very general parallels to the others (cf. above, page 73). Sayings attributed to Jesus in the gospels have, it seems, become part of the general stock-in-trade of Christian teachers, who used them without acknowledgement. But the possibility cannot be ruled out that the reverse process has occurred, and that maxims in general use, from whatever source, have been mistakenly attributed to Jesus. Matthew 6:34 and 7:6 have been interpreted in this way.

(b) Matthew 7:22 refers to those who prophesy in the name of Jesus, and this is supported by references elsewhere to the activity of prophets in the life of the congregations, especially in worship (e.g. Acts 13:1f., I Corinthians 14). Apparently they spoke in the name of the risen Lord, that is, on his behalf. He was believed to be speaking through them (cf. especially Revelation 22:16 and 18). Were such sayings treasured as much as those of the earthly Jesus? Was any real distinction made between them, when both types of saying were felt to express the mind of the Lord who had now risen and still presided over his disciples? If the distinction was not sharply drawn, what was to prevent a saying of the Lord, delivered through a prophet, being attributed to the Lord in his earthly ministry? An example of such a 'prophetic' word is given in Revelation 3:20. It comes in a 'book of prophecy' (22:18), written by one who was 'in the spirit' (that is, inspired to prophesy, 1:10). 'Here I stand knocking at the door; if anyone hears my voice and opens the door, I will come in and sit down to supper with him and he with me.' Compare Matthew 18:20, for a saying in a similar style. Although it refers, not to the time of Jesus' ministry, but to the period after the resurrection, the present tense is used, and not, as we might expect, the future: 'Where two or three have met together in my name, I am there among them.' It is difficult to resist the conclusion that this saying too originated in Christian prophecy. Still more likely is Matthew 28:19, for it is difficult to explain the early church's practice of baptizing in the name of Jesus alone (Acts 2:38), or their hesitation in extending baptism to Gentiles, to which both Acts and Paul's letters bear witness, if Jesus had in fact given explicit instructions to baptize all nations in the name of the Trinity as early as the period shortly after his resurrection.

(c) We have already noted the importance of the Old Testament in the thought of the New, and the fact that it provided an important key for interpreting the death and resurrection of Jesus as the will of God (cf. above, page 91). So in the gospels (especially Matthew and John) our attention is often drawn to Scriptures fulfilled in details of the story of Jesus. How far have Old Testament passages actually shaped the way the story is told, and even led to incidents being invented in fulfilment of them, because of the conviction that prophecy must be fulfilled? All the gospels, for example, mention the soldiers dicing for Jesus' clothes at the crucifixion. Only John 19:24 refers to Psalm 22:18 being fulfilled, and distinguishes the treatment of different garments, leading us to suspect that the story has been embellished with greater detail to make it a more explicit fulfilment of Scripture. But the other gospels, while not mentioning the psalm, all echo its language in their description of the incident, and if we did not have evidence that it was a regular practice for the execution party at a crucifixion to take possession of the convict's clothes, we might suspect that the whole episode had grown out of the psalm. Similarly Matthew 21:1-11 has Jesus riding on two animals, on account of this gospel's interpretation of Zechariah 9:9 (where only one animal is intended, as the other gospels realize). So much for any concern for historical realism!

112

Thus, in connexion with both teaching and narrative, there are grounds for saying that influences were at work in the life of the church which make it difficult for us at this late stage to establish beyond all question that a given saying or narrative has been preserved intact. It is not even clear that at the time the gospels were written an investigation could have been carried out which would have established it. The modifications we have been considering were probably largely unconscious. Moreover, what the use of the Old Testament particularly suggests is that there was a fundamental difference between our approach to history and that of the New Testament writers. We begin by asking what happened and then try to interpret it; they began with a theological conviction concerning what ought to happen, and then concluded (because God directs events) that it did. All this has to be set against the evidence we saw in previous chapters which suggested that neither the gospel writers nor their predecessors in oral tradition felt that they had an entirely free hand with the traditions they inherited, much as they might have adapted them.

We are thus brought to the distinction, of which much has been made in the last two hundred years, between Jesus as the church since the resurrection has believed in him and Jesus as he would have appeared to an observer before the crucifixion; or, to use the conventional terms, between the 'Christ of faith' and the 'Jesus of history'. The distinction is in fact much older. Early Christian writers often had to combat allegations that the disciples in their preaching about Jesus' resurrection and divinity had concealed the historical truth. In the nineteenth century however it became common to explain away the supernatural elements in the gospels (miracles, heavenly voices and the like) by distinguishing between 'what really happened' and the 'naïve and credulous' accounts of the events given by the disciples. The distinction could be used to discredit Christian origins, as in the claim that the disciples invented the story of the resurrection for their own ends, hiding the body of Jesus to substantiate it. It could also be used to advocate a reform of Christianity. A favourite version, associated with the name of A. Harnack (1851–1930), was that Jesus preached a universal message of the fatherhood of God and the brotherhood of man, while the church invested him in the theological garments of divinity and

113

atonement, and hung about the neck of his followers the burden of an institutional church. But in essence the distinction is simply the admission that the New Testament presentation of Jesus and the historical truth about him are not necessarily the same thing, and for nearly two hundred years a major concern of critical scholarship has been the effort to establish what that historical truth was – the so-called 'quest of the historical Jesus'.

An influential body of opinion regards such a quest as illegitimate, representing a misunderstanding of the New Testament and a betrayal of Christian faith. In the last fifty years this view has had a powerful advocate in the person of Rudolf Bultmann, although some of his pupils have swung to a moderating position. It has usually been maintained in combination with an understanding of Christianity in existentialist terms, to which we shall return in chapter 11. In the New Testament, it is argued, the risen Jesus is the centre of interest. Many parts of it make no mention of his life and ministry, referring only to his cross and resurrection, and to his glory, present and future. Even the gospels really speak of the risen Jesus and make no attempt to detach the historical Jesus from him. Neither should we. If we succeeded in recovering the Jesus of history, he would not be the Christ whom the early church knew. Further, it is contended, faith should not be propped up by historical supports, for that destroys its essential quality. Faith, to be faith, must not depend on anything but God. If we try to construct a historical portrait of Jesus, the danger is that we shall use it as a substitute for faith, as a proof that the church's message is true. Faith can exist only where there is no proof. In any case, if we are seeking proof in the fruits of historical research we shall be disappointed, for the history of scholarship shows how unreliable scholars' opinions are, offering only a kaleidoscope of shifting hypotheses and tentative conclusions. Academic research cannot have theological importance.

There is much in this view to commend it. As we noted earlier, the aim in pursuing the historical Jesus has often been the reformer's object of getting back to the true gospel and liberating it from the distortions imposed by the church. It is a welcome reaction to assert that it is precisely the church's faith (in its earlier forms, as preserved in the New Testament, at least) and not the historical figure which lies at the centre of Christianity.

114

Some will also welcome an attitude which gives Christian faith security against being undermined by critical scholarship. For once the step has been taken of saying that it does not matter what the historical Jesus was like, we are free to keep our faith in the exalted Lord, undisturbed by historical doubts of any kind.

Many however will feel that the price is too high. Can we really say that the historical truth about Jesus does not matter for faith? What if the message of the early church were a confidence trick on a huge scale, or the belief in the resurrection a stupid blunder, based on the evidence of women who merely visited the wrong tomb? What if Jesus never even existed? In any case it is far from clear that the New Testament writers were so completely lacking in interest in the historical Jesus: always he is taken for granted. Even in the epistles the message of the resurrection has of necessity a backward reference: it is the crucified Jesus who was raised. The message of the cross similarly presupposes that which preceded it. Crucifixion of itself was hardly news in the ancient world, being a common and over-employed form of execution. It gained its significance in Christian preaching from the identity of the One who suffered it. So there was always an implication that Jesus was an innocent and godly (in biblical terms, righteous) man, even when it was not explicitly mentioned. Furthermore, we do have the gospels: four documents which are evidence that in some quarters at least it was felt appropriate to present the message about Jesus in terms of what he had done and said.

It is therefore false to the New Testament to elevate the distinction between the Jesus of history and the Christ of faith into a dichotomy. We have insisted that the distinction must be admitted, and the Jesus of history is certainly no substitute for the Christ of faith, but if there is no connexion between the two, the Christ of faith, losing all real reference to a historical figure, must become merely a convenient term for a set of religious convictions which could equally well be known by some other name. This would indeed be a betrayal of Christianity of the kind we are urged to avoid. It is the relation between the historical events and what Christians believe about them which is the crucial question; and it follows that critical studies must have an unsettling effect upon faith. We cannot insulate faith; if traditional Christianity is right in asserting that God has revealed himself in a historical person, faith must be vulnerable to the results of historical enquiry.

Such an enquiry, however, is not easy to undertake. Virtually everything we know about Jesus comes to us through the filter of the church's faith in him. Evidence about Jesus from non-Christian sources, taken by itself, is negligible, beyond assuring us that he lived, was crucified under Pontius Pilate and was believed to have risen again. We have to rely chiefly on the gospels, and if they are the only window available to us through which to view the Jesus of history, we are left with the question how, if at all, we can bypass their distortions.

Of course total scepticism is illogical. If the gospels obscured the truth about Jesus completely, we should be unable to detect the fact. We might choose to accept their account outright or reject it, but it would be on dogmatic grounds, not on any evidence. Only because at some points the gospels allow us to see another picture beneath the surface of their own can we assert that such a picture existed, and differed from what has been superimposed upon it. We encounter major difficulties, however, when we try to establish an agreed method by which to separate the original from the overlay.

(a) Some, for example, have argued that vividness of narrative is a sign that the narrative in question is based upon an *eye-witness report*. But such vividness is also present both in some of the parables, which are not supposed to describe actual events, and in the apocryphal gospels, which are agreed to be fictional. In fact it has been argued to the contrary that vividness and elaboration, such as the addition of the characters' names (compare John 18:10f. with the other gospels), is a sign of lateness. This is hardly more satisfactory. Certainly later gospels abound with names which are probably fictional, but some names in the canonical gospels must be genuine, and unless we believe that all happenings are simple, it does not follow that the simplest stories (any more than the most vivid) are necessarily the most original (cf. above, page 71). In fact no infallible criterion for an eye-witness report exists, and in any case (as is well known) eye-witnesses can be mistaken or prejudiced, or see only part of the action. An eye-witness source does not guarantee historicity.

(b) Similarly the presence of *details consonant with what we know of life in Palestine,* and references to historical events or political and administrative conditions of the time, and the possibility of translating sayings back to Aramaic, all point to a Palestinian origin for the tradition concerned. But this does not of itself prove that the tradition takes us back to Jesus; it may have originated in the Palestinian church. On the other hand, while it is very likely that Jesus spoke a dialect of Aramaic, we are far from knowing all the limitations and possibilities of that language; nor is it impossible, according to some experts, that Jesus may on occasions have used Hebrew, or even a little Greek, although it remains true that the presence of details impossible to reconcile with a Palestinian setting point to a different origin.

(c) A more important test is the so-called *criterion of dissimilarity.* If a saying is so unlike both what we know of contemporary Judaism and the beliefs of the later church that it cannot be accounted for as a conventional Jewish or Christian idea which has slipped into the tradition about Jesus, then it must have come from Jesus himself. By this means at least some elements in the gospels can be asserted to have originated with Jesus and a valuable contribution has been made to our knowledge by it. But even this test is limited. It assumes (perhaps rightly) that Jesus was the only really original thinker behind the gospel tradition; often the further assumption is made that Jesus never said anything that was *not* original. Not surprisingly the use of this criterion produces a Jesus strikingly at variance both with his contemporaries and with the later church, for it identifies only those points on which he differed from both groups, not what he had in common with them. In practice no one applies this test rigorously, for all assume he shared some Jewish ideas, such as the doctrine of God.

(d) In conjunction with this last test the *criterion of coherence* is also used. If a saying fails to pass the criterion of dissimilarity it may nevertheless be treated as a saying of Jesus, if it is compatible with other sayings whose authenticity can be demonstrated. It exhibits his 'style' and may be used to illustrate his teaching. Strictly the use of this criterion is illogical, for if one saying can be admitted on these grounds, in spite of failing the dissimilarity test, why not another to which no authentic parallel happens to have survived? Nevertheless this test does provide

117

some sayings which may indicate common ground between Jesus and his contemporaries or his later followers, and which may broaden the body of teaching we are prepared to treat as authentic.

(e) A further criterion is the *criterion of multiple attestation*. When many lines of evidence converge, from different sources and different types of tradition, then we are in touch with a characteristic of the historical Jesus. Thus many sayings in all four gospels stress love as typical of his teaching. It is also a theme of many stories about him. Therefore, although an emphasis on love is to be found in some other Jewish teachers, and was certainly part of the church's teaching, it is difficult to believe that it was not also part of the teaching of Jesus. This is a more positive test which helps us to see some continuity between Jesus and the church, but it is very general. It shows us the broad themes of his teaching, without necessarily authenticating a particular saying or incident.

In all these tests we are hampered by the difficulty of our comparative ignorance of the world in which Jesus lived. We depend on our ability to identify Greek ideas and later Christian interests and to specify what was commonplace in Judaism at the time. A major discovery of contemporary Jewish documents, such as occurred in the finding of the Dead Sea Scrolls, may lead to a considerable shift in our estimation of what ideas are likely to have been held in a Palestinian setting in the first century. This is equally true of our interpretation of events. If for example we knew more about criminal procedures at the time, we should be able to settle some controversial questions about the trial of Jesus, such as whether both hearings, before Caiaphas and Pilate, actually occurred, or whether the Jewish trial was (as some have argued) a fiction of Christian apologists in an attempt to shift the blame for the crucifixion from the Romans, who were historically responsible, to the Jews.

It is not surprising, in view of these difficulties, that it has proved impossible to produce a detailed account of the Jesus of history which will win general assent. Not only do scholars dispute the interpretation of particular items of evidence; they differ radically on what counts as evidence. Further, from the same data in the gospels they may produce quite different results, because of their estimate of the bearing upon the interpretation of them of non-biblical evidence, or of developments in the New Testament church.

In practice not every element in the gospels is equally contested. There is no doubt that Jesus actually lived, was crucified under Pontius Pilate and was at least believed to have risen from the dead. Theories, once popular, which made him out to be a myth are today generally dismissed as wild. Of course attempts are still made along these lines from time to time, but we must concern ourselves with the mainstream of serious work on the subject. Similarly there is a wide measure of agreement that a major theme of Jesus' preaching was the kingdom of God, that he taught by parables, and that he caused offence by ignoring religious convention in his contacts with moral and social outcasts.

The main areas of dispute can be summarized under three headings:

(a) How much do we know for certain about the course of Jesus' life? Some treat the outline of Mark's gospel as historical, others regard it as a pattern devised for theological or teaching purposes. Some accept individual narratives, including the stories of the virginity of Mary, Jesus' birth in Bethlehem, his baptism, transfiguration, all his miracles (not just the healings), and his bodily resurrection from the tomb, as describing events which actually happened; others regard some or all of them as expressions of Christian faith in narrative form.

(b) How far can we recover the precise words of his teaching? Some would regard most of the sayings in the synoptic gospels as genuine; others would discriminate between them, assigning them to various stages in the development of oral tradition, and holding of the earliest stage only that it is the earliest form of the tradition we possess, without pronouncing on the question whether it accurately represents the teaching of Jesus.

(c) How does Jesus fit into the Jewish background? Is he best seen as an unconventional rabbi or teacher, as a prophet, as a messianic deliverer, as a martyr-figure witnessing for God against the ungodly, or is his distinctiveness that he fits none of these categories? What attitude did he take to the widespread expectation of his contemporaries of a dramatic, imminent end to the present world-order brought about by an act of God, and how far should his preaching about the Kingdom be seen in these terms? What was his own estimate of himself? Was he conscious of being the Messiah, or the Son of God, or the Son of Man? What, if any or all of these titles are authentic, did he understand by them, since each is capable of a variety of meanings? How did he interpret his impending death, if in fact he foresaw its occurrence at all? Did he anticipate his resurrection, and an indefinite future after it, and provide for this by inaugurating the church, or did he expect a speedy end which would make a continuing organization of his disciples unnecessary? It will not escape the reader that these questions touch precisely on those aspects of the gospels which affect the central themes of Christian belief – who Jesus is, what he has achieved, and the significance of the church.

It is important to notice that many of the disputed points concern details. Those who insist that no single narrative of Jesus healing the sick can be treated as an eye-witness report of an actual incident may nevertheless argue that the number of such stories we possess shows, together with certain sayings referring to healings, that Jesus certainly was accustomed to heal the sick, and their many common features give us a good general idea of the way he went about it. While we may not be able to give absolute proof that particular sayings are original, we may be able to pick out many of the salient themes of his preaching, and even some characteristics of his way of speaking. If we have few of his actual words (his *ipsissima verba*), we may yet be able to pick out his actual style of speech (his *ipsissima vox*).

There are in fact two levels at which a historical enquiry may be conducted: the particular and the general. At the particular level there is the question whether an event did or did not happen as described. Sometimes it is possible to prove it beyond reasonable doubt; often the evidence is insufficient, and we may have to suspend judgement, or in some cases accept it as credible, though not capable of proof, because it fits into a general pattern. Very few of the events in the gospels are capable of proof in the strict sense because there is not enough corroborative evidence. At the general level we are less concerned with particular events, although they cannot be ignored altogether. Our main concern is the assessment of a person, the characteristics of an age, or the main features of a movement. In such questions precise dates and geographical locations may matter little. We may not be able to describe a single day's events exactly, or vouch for more than half a person's recorded utterances, yet we may have an impression of his character, the effect he had on his contemporaries and his influence on subsequent events. It is important in the case of Jesus to be clear at what level our questions are asked. Much of the controversy about Jesus is at the level of the particular. At the general level there is more agreement.

Furthermore, a rigorously critical approach to the gospels may lead to some unexpected conclusions. It has been pointed out that the way God is addressed in Jesus' teaching simply as 'Father', in the Lord's Prayer and elsewhere, is unique in Jewish literature in its directness and intimacy, and that many of the sayings and traditions of his activity imply an assumption of authority and independence of human traditions which is without parallel in Judaism. All this suggests that, whether or not Jesus used of himself any of the titles of honour (such as Messiah) which the church later adopted to describe him, he did assume that he was destined to play an unprecedented role in God's dealings with the world, a role which it was the later function of the church's faith to describe. This is the approach adopted by the so-called 'new quest of the historical Jesus', and for its findings some have coined the term 'implicit Christology', in contrast to the explicit Christology, or doctrine about Christ's person, of the Christian confessions of faith.

The importance of the last three paragraphs must be underlined. A significant development in recent discussion of the search for the historical truth about Jesus has been the growing recognition that the goal must be re-defined. During the nineteenth century it was generally assumed that the aim of historical enquiry was to give a purely objective account of the facts. It was thought to be analogous to the natural sciences as they were then viewed. Part of its appeal was that it promised escape from subjective opinions and theological controversy into a world of detached calm where truth alone mattered and was sought with rigorous dedication. It was therefore assumed that, if only agreement on methods could be reached, the 'real truth' about Jesus could be recovered. We now recognize that this was a characteristically nineteenth-century ideal. It was not the spirit in which the gospels were written, for they are avowedly confessions of faith (cf. John 20:31). Nor is it an attainable ideal. Even in

121

relation to the natural sciences absolute detachment is impossible; still less is it possible in the study of history. Of course facts are facts: either Julius Caesar was murdered on the Ides of March 44 BC or he was not – although establishing whether some events actually occurred often depends more on judgement and probability than the layman imagines. But how does one establish 'facts' about character and motive? Why was Caesar murdered? Did his death rid the world of a menace, or deprive it of a benefactor? Scholars still dispute these questions, and one cannot begin to answer them without revealing one's own temperament and political views, for one is making a character-judgement based upon complex and ambiguous evidence, part of which is provided by Caesar's contemporaries who were not impartial themselves. There are even cases where the historian's decision about whether an event actually occurred will depend upon prior decisions about a person's character and the likelihood of his having done what is attributed to him. All historical judgements, particularly about personalities, involve some elements of prejudice, although a good historian will always try to recognize and allow for its effect on his thinking.

In the case of Jesus additional factors complicate the issue. The historian who is a Christian believer will try to be as impartial as the next man, but it would be surprising if, as a believer he did not hope that the result of his enquiries would be a Jesus who was worthy of faith. In particular problems arise in connexion with the supernatural element in the gospels. The historian is accustomed to studying human activity. He will of course allow for the possibility of the unusual; for example, he may allow that certain individuals are endowed with unusual sensitivity to what is going on in the minds of others, or with uncanny powers of foreseeing the future. Different historians may have different views on the limits of these possibilities, but all will agree that there are limits. If someone is reported to have walked through a solid brick wall, leaving it intact, every historian is likely to regard the report as false. Unless he assumes the normal rules of what is possible he cannot make a historical study at all. He must be able to distinguish true from false.

But in the gospels the supernatural plays an important part. Was Jesus the son of a virgin? Did he walk on water, or rise from the dead? Did the shepherds see angels at his birth? Some

122

readers regard these traditions as a way of expressing religious convictions about Jesus in story form. Others approach the gospels with the conviction that, since Jesus was divine he was capable of feats surpassing normal human capabilities, but if the historian once accepts this, he surrenders the possibility of making a historical study. He must deal with Jesus as a human being, and leave faith to build on the foundations in whatever way it can. He can assess the strength of the historical traditions of the virgin birth, the resurrection or Jesus' claim to divinity, but he cannot as a historian prove these traditions to be justified. In this respect he is not a substitute for the gospels with their presentation of what faith sees in Jesus. This however is not to suggest that historical enquiry should be abandoned; only that its limitations should be recognized. The gospels with their 'unhistorical, partisan' approach in this respect present us with the truth about the past better than the historian.

There is no doubt that modern scholarship has shown us that we know less about Jesus than we once thought we did. The gospels are not biographies of Jesus in the modern sense of the word, and do not provide sufficient evidence for us to write one now. It is doubtful however whether the position is any different with any other figures of the distant past who have left no writings of their own. On any showing we know more about Jesus than about most of his disciples or any of his opponents. Many of the limitations of our knowledge apply to all historical study. The complicating factor is that Jesus is also an object of religious faith. Here modern scholarship has highlighted the fact that if we are looking for knowledge of the Jesus of history, which will form an adequate foundation for Christian faith, there is no way in which we can bypass the testimony of his first believers. Impartial enquiry can reassure us on certain points. It can show that there are no grounds for suspecting deceitful falsification of the record. But if we are to go beyond this we must accept that to believe in Jesus means, now as always in Christian history, to believe the testimony of those who, in New Testament times, wrote of him as they believed in him.

10. Objections
in a Historical Context

In the Introduction to this book we took note of some of the objections which are commonly raised against the critical study of the New Testament. We suggested a reply to one of them in the first chapter, when we showed that the concerns of critical scholarship arise out of the problems which present themselves in any intelligent reading of the New Testament itself. The Bible, we saw, is an ancient book, and like others of its age needs explanation. The other objections we deferred until we had had the opportunity of watching the scholar at work on these problems. In this chapter we return to a consideration of them, and it will help to set our answers in perspective if we begin with a brief thumbnail sketch of the history of New Testament scholarship. Clearly no more than this can be attempted in the space available, and it will necessarily be very selective.

We shall divide the story into periods, noting the preoccupations, the leading figures and the dominant schools of thought in each. Of course it is not a story of simple progress in a straight line, or even, like the making of a jig-saw, of the addition of pieces in different places over a wide area until the whole is complete. It is more like the history of a war, with many battles being fought simultaneously on many fronts, advance at one point, retreat at another, many apparently successful incursions ultimately failing, while other single-handed skirmishes turn out in the end to be the spearhead of advance. While only the outstanding developments tend to be recorded, they would be nothing without much painstaking effort over the whole field.

Biblical scholarship as we now know it is a phenomenon of the last two centuries. The first tentative steps are usually attributed to Richard Simon (1638–1712), whose main contribution to New Testament study concerned textual criticism. But some of his work was suppressed by authority, and he remained at that time a lone figure. In the eighteenth century there were a few others, including J. J. Wettstein (1693–1754) and J. J. Griesbach (1745–1812) who between them laid the foundations for modern study of the text, Griesbach also being important for his work on the synoptic problem. But it was in the late eighteenth century that the movement really got under way with Hermann Reimarus (1694–1768), sections of whose work, *Apology on behalf of the Reasonable Worshippers of God*, were published after his death by G. E. Lessing in 1774–8, and are generally known as the *Wolfenbüttel Fragments*. He held that Jesus sought to bring in by political revolution the kingdom of God which his contemporaries expected, and failing to do so, was crucified by the Romans. His disciples gave his death a new, spiritual significance, stealing his body from the grave and putting about the story of the resurrection and expectation of his return. Reimarus' theories, which caused a storm of protest, are important not for themselves but because he was the first to insist that Jesus must be understood in the light of the Jewish ideas of his time, and that a distinction should be made between his own message and that of his disciples.

Reimarus' work led directly to the work of the nineteenth century. Eight names are outstanding in this period, two in the first half of the century and the rest towards the end. D. F. Strauss (1808–74) of Tübingen published the first edition of his *Life of Jesus* in 1835. In it he tried to break through the shortcomings of the two approaches to the gospels then current, the conservative approach which treated them literally throughout, and the rationalist which tried to explain away the supernatural elements in accordance with contemporary scientific ideas. Strauss saw that the rationalist approach left an account of Jesus so trivial that it was impossible to explain why the gospels were ever written. He sought an alternative explanation in myth: the gospels are evidence of what the disciples believed about Jesus, in the form of stories or myths about him, which are more important for the modern student than any historical kernel behind them.

The reputation of F. C. Baur (1792–1860), also of Tübingen, rests not on a single work but on a series of studies, and on the influence he exercised over a number of scholars who continued to work on similar lines and came to be known as the Tübingen

125

school. In its final form the position of this school was that no book of the New Testament can be fully understood unless its place within the development of early Christianity has been recognized. Early Christianity was marked – as the letters of Paul were held to show – by a sharp conflict between the Jewish-Christian party of Peter and James and the Gentile-Christian party of Paul, which later writings (especially the book of Acts) attempted to gloss over, in order to pave the way for a harmonious future. Baur insisted on the importance of recognizing the tendency of a particular writing, that is, the point of view it is intended to uphold, in order both to determine its date and to detect the distortion of history which the tendency has produced. On this basis, in Baur's view, only Romans, I and II Corinthians and Galatians of Paul's letters are genuine; only Matthew among the gospels is early, while many parts of the New Testament which display reconciling tendencies are to be dated well into the second century.

In their general view Strauss and Baur and their followers undoubtedly went too far. They pushed their theories beyond the point where they could be supported by the evidence. Their influence has been decisive, however, not only because of the reactions they provoked, but because many of their insights have stood the test of time and are reflected in modern work.

Much of the immediate reaction to the Tübingen scholars was negative, but a few outstanding nineteenth-century figures are best interpreted as reacting in a positive way to their challenge. B. F. Westcott (1825–1901), J. B. Lightfoot (1828–89) and F. J. A. Hort (1828–92), perhaps the best trio of contemporary scholars Britain has ever had, did much to win acceptance for a critical approach to the Bible by the way they combined it with theological orthodoxy. Apart from a series of commentaries to which all contributed, Westcott and Hort's major work was a printed edition of the Greek New Testament which gathered up the fruits of previous textual study, and remains the starting-point for all further work; while Lightfoot, by a thorough study of the early history of the church in the first two centuries, cleared the way for a much more accurate picture of early Christian developments than had been possible in Baur's time, and refuted some of Baur's theories of excessively late dating for some parts of the New Testament.

126

A reaction of a different kind came from Adolf Harnack (1851–1930), a church historian as well as New Testament scholar. We have already referred to his general view of Jesus and the development of Christianity (see above, page 113), which he set out in popular form in 1900 in *The Essence of Christianity*. Fundamentally Harnack divorces Jesus and the early church from their historical setting as decisively as earlier critics like Reimarus and Baur had tied them to it. Although expressed within Jewish forms, the teaching of Jesus according to Harnack is both timeless and simple, the fatherhood of God and the infinite value of the human soul. At the time Harnack's influence was immense, and there are still many who are sympathetic to his 'Liberal-Protestant' antagonism to the institutional church and its developed theology, but he is more important today for the fact that it is against his position that much twentieth-century scholarship still reacts.

The name of Johannes Weiss (1863–1914) will always be associated with eschatology (a term variously used to mean the doctrine of the last things, beliefs about the end of the world or, as here, an emphasis on the imminence of the end of all things). In *The Preaching of Jesus Concerning the Kingdom of God*, published in 1892, he reasserted the view that Jesus must be understood in the light of the Judaism of his time, and in particular that the kingdom of God in his preaching meant not, as in modern ideas, God's rule in the heart of the individual nor a world-wide utopia for which men are called to work, but a wholly future new world, brought about by God alone, ushered in by conflict with the powers of evil, the resurrection of the dead and the day of judgement. This kingdom Jesus proclaimed to be imminent. Although Weiss' 'thoroughgoing eschatology' has been modified by much later work, he has made a lasting impact upon New Testament studies because none would now deny the eschatological perspective in the teaching of Jesus and throughout the New Testament.

A. Jülicher (1857–1938) was mentioned in our discussion of parables (see above, page 77), and we do not need to repeat what was said there, but he deserves to be included in our survey at this point because his book *The Parables of Jesus* (1888–99), surprisingly never translated into English, has had a very wide influence, as is still evident in the most important modern book

127

on the parables, by J. Jeremias (1947), which combines the insights of Jülicher and Weiss. Jülicher himself did not appreciate the importance of eschatology.

The nineteenth century witnessed the full flowering of New Testament scholarship. By the end of the century the foundations had been laid in practically every department of New Testament study. The documents had been analysed in detail and the basic questions about their authorship, date and genuineness opened up. John's gospel had been recognized as being on a different footing from the others, and the synoptic problem had been stated, although not resolved. The questions which Reimarus had first asked about the historical reliability of the New Testament and particularly about the relationship between Jesus and Judaism on the one hand and the later church (especially Paul) on the other, had been answered in a variety of ways. On the text and the Canon, too, the definitive lines for future work had been laid down. As a result, by 1900 scholars had reliable tools to work with: accurate concordances, a printed text based on sound principles, an immense accumulation of detailed information in commentaries and dictionaries, and the first translations of the New Testament based on these researches.

The most important achievement however was that scholarship had won the right to exist, at least in the Protestant world. Some of Simon's work had been suppressed, and others suffered the same fate. Strenuous battles had to be fought before church and state leaders generally recognized the legitimacy of the new approach. It was largely due to men like Lightfoot, Westcott and Hort that it was accepted that critical scholarship was compatible with Christian faith. The twentieth century has not witnessed in Protestantism the same pressures against the academic freedom of biblical scholars as were exerted before.

The first decade of the twentieth century is marked by two important figures and two great movements. Albert Schweitzer (1875–1965) captured the imagination with his dramatic renunciation of an academic career for the life of a medical missionary in Africa. He is important in New Testament studies both for his monumental review of all previous attempts to write a life of Jesus (*The Quest of the Historical Jesus*, 1906), and by his insistence that both Jesus and Paul must be interpreted in the light of 'thoroughgoing eschatology'. In the case of Jesus this

128

meant interpreting him as proclaiming an imminent end to the world and, when this expectation was not fulfilled, deliberately going to Jerusalem to suffer in the hope of bringing it about.

W. Wrede (1859–1906), though slightly earlier, exercises a greater influence than Schweitzer at the present time. He can justly be claimed as the father of redaction criticism (although he did not use the term), and of all those who emphasize the influence of Christian belief in the portrait of Jesus in the gospels. In 1901, in *The Messianic Secret in the Gospels*, he insisted that Jesus' emphasis on secrecy particularly in Mark's gospel is not historical but the product of the beliefs of the evangelists and their predecessors, who read back their own understanding of Jesus as Messiah into his earthly life and at the same time tried to account for the fact that he was not recognized as such at the time.

The first of the movements is generally known as the 'history-of-religions school', of which the leading figures were R. Reitzenstein (1861–1931) and W. Bousset (1865–1920). They were much impressed by the similarities between the New Testament and the teaching and practices of many of the pagan religious groups of the time, which they claimed as evidence of the influence of pagan ideas upon Christianity as, with the growing number of Gentile converts, it developed out of its original Jewish environment. They overstated their case, both because they paid insufficient attention to the date of the documents they cited in evidence, and because they did not give due weight to differences as well as similarities, but they did press the question, to which we still seek the final answer, of the origin of New Testament teaching in its various forms, and the influences at work in the minds of the early Christians.

Catholic modernism was a movement of a different kind. Beginning about 1890, it was an attempt by a number of Roman Catholic scholars, notably A. Loisy (1857–1940), to adopt a critical approach to the Bible and to express Catholic doctrine in the light of contemporary thought. Their intention was to defend the faith against attacks on it by Liberal Protestants and others, but from the point of view of the more conservative they conceded too much, and the movement was condemned in 1907 and many of its leaders excommunicated. This was followed by a series of rulings by the Pontifical Biblical Commission on such matters as the historical accuracy and apostolic authorship of Matthew's and John's gospels, and the Pauline authorship of Hebrews, as well as a number of pronouncements on the Old Testament. Present-day Roman Catholics argue that there were pastoral reasons for the clamp-down, because of the effect of modernism on the faith of ordinary Christians, but there is no doubt that the official reaction prevented effective Roman Catholic participation in the work of scholarship for fifty years, to great loss on both sides.

Between the two world wars two names dominated the scene. Karl Barth (1886–1968) published his *Commentary on Romans* in 1919. Barth's primary importance is as a theologian, but his *Commentary* has widely influenced New Testament scholars far beyond the ranks of those who would consider themselves as Barthian in theology. His essential plea was to allow the Bible to speak in its own terms. He was struck by the extent to which previous scholars (Strauss, Baur, Harnack, for example) had allowed their own outlook and philosophical presuppositions to determine their understanding of the Bible. It is not for us to decide on the basis of our ideas what is true and false in the biblical message; rather we must listen to the Word of God and allow it to judge our preconceptions. The protest was timely; but the real question is whether such influence can ultimately be avoided, and whether Barth himself does not equally see the Bible through his own spectacles.

Barth's influence can best be seen in the 'biblical theology' movement, which has lasted until the sixties. Many scholars, including E. C. Hoskyns (1884–1937), A. Richardson (1905–75), and O. Cullmann (born 1902), insisting that the Bible should be allowed to speak in its own terms have pointed to the uniqueness of its message in the ancient world. In the New Testament they have tended to stress the influence of the Old Testament, rather than Greek and oriental ideas. Today it may be questioned whether the unity of the Bible was not over-stressed and its diversity ignored, and whether too little weight was given to the links between the biblical communities and their environment, but at the time it was an important corrective. One lasting monument to its influence, although certainly not merely a manifesto of the movement, is the enormous *Theological Dictionary of the New Testament* edited by G. Kittel and

G. Friedrich, which was begun in 1928 and took forty-five years to complete. Its nine volumes bring together a wealth of material on the background of the key theological words in the New Testament with a discussion of the interpretation of important passages, and is a major reference work.

The other great figure of the period between the wars, and after, is R. Bultmann (1884–1976). Bultmann is best known as one of the pioneers in the use of form criticism in the New Testament, and for his generally sceptical attitude to the historical value of the gospels as evidence for the life of Jesus. But his contribution has not been confined to these topics. On the one hand he has insisted (in the tradition of the history-of-religions school) that much New Testament theology can be understood only in the light of the influence of the Gnostic movement, which he believes is not just a phenomenon of the late first and the second centuries onward in which Christian ideas became diluted with a variety of pagan ones, but an originally non-Christian, oriental religious movement, which took a variety of forms and whose language and ideas were taken over by New Testament writers (particularly in the gospel of John) as a vehicle of expression for Christianity. To this source he would trace the doctrine of a heavenly redeemer who descends to earth and returns to heaven, the distinctively Christian element being the cross. Post-war discoveries of Gnostic manuscripts have reopened the question of the origins of the movement, and the matter cannot be settled until they have all been published and studied.

The other main issue with which Bultmann has been associated is the question of 'demythologizing', to which we shall turn in the next chapter. Again the influence of earlier scholars should be noted (cf. Strauss). While few British scholars have been very sympathetic to the existentialist element in Bultmann's work, none would deny the importance of the question he has raised.

Five issues have dominated the years since the Second World War, most of which we have discussed already and need only mention now. Biblical theology continued to flourish until the sixties. Redaction criticism arose after the war and is now a major preoccupation in the study of the gospels. The debate on hermeneutics (which we shall introduce in the next chapter) continues, and there has been a movement back to the question of the historical Jesus, considered now within the framework of form criticism (the so-called 'New Quest'). The other major factor has been the growing participation of Roman Catholics. Beginning from a papal encyclical of 1943 (*Divino Afflante Spiritu*), but particularly since the Second Vatican Council (Constitution on Divine Revelation, *Dei Verbum*, 1965), Catholic scholars have begun to make a major contribution to critical study, using the same methods and coming to similar conclusions as others. At the same time they are more frequently reminded of the pastoral implications of their work, that is, the need to see it in the wider context of the life of the church, and it may well be that this awareness of responsibility will in future help to protect the scholarly community from some of the fads and excesses of the past.

Meanwhile the spade work goes on; literally, as archaeological discoveries continue to bring new evidence to light. The finding of Jewish writings in the caves around Qumran on the shores of the Dead Sea since 1947 and a library of Gnostic documents at Nag Hammadi near Luxor in Egypt about the same time have thrown a flood of new light on the Jewish world at the time of Jesus and on the environment of the early church in the two centuries which followed. At another level we may mention the continuing work of comparing the New Testament with later Jewish writings, as exemplified in H. Strack and P. Billerbeck's *Commentary on the New Testament in the Light of Talmud and Midrash* (1922–61). The results of detailed work on particular problems are utilized in more general works on New Testament theology, literature, or history, and in commentaries on individual books. International contact between scholars increases, as one might expect with better travel facilities, and daily it seems research work becomes more specialized and more restricted in range as the number of researchers in various countries increases.

In the light of this necessarily sketchy survey let us now turn to some of the objections which were raised in our first chapter. (1) We will begin with the objection that modern scholarship is a late development, which the church showed over a long period that she could do without. We have seen that it did not really get under way until the late eighteenth century. If we were able to understand the Bible for so long without it, why do we need it now?

First, we must insist that the Bible has never been an open book which presented no problems. As early as the third century AD writers were beginning to discuss problems of variant manuscript readings, discrepancies between books and problems of authorship, and might have done more if it had not been for the limitations of the knowledge available at the time. But the clearest proof that the Bible has always been problematical is the church's use from the very earliest times of allegorical interpretation.

Allegorical interpretation starts from the admission that the text is unintelligible as it stands. The literal meaning is too obscure, too absurd, or perhaps too trivial, to be the real meaning intended by God, and the interpreter is required in consequence to seek another meaning hidden beneath it. The words of the text then become a code by which a concealed spiritual truth is conveyed, and their unintelligibility at the literal level is regarded as the clue given by God that a deeper meaning is present. Thus Origen, who died about AD 250, argued that at the temptation of Jesus the devil could not possibly have taken him to a mountain high enough literally to see all the kingdoms of the world with the physical eye. 'Events which did not take place at all are woven into the records of what literally did happen.' Rather the devil reminded Christ of the kingdom which really belongs to him, and not of earthly rulers, Persians, Indians, etc., but of the vices and misery which hold sway in it. Similarly, the people in Numbers 23:24 who are like a lion which 'does not lie down until it devours the prey and drinks the blood of the slain' are the church which eats the flesh and drinks the blood of Christ in the sacrament.

In pre-Christian times Greek philosophers had used the allegorical method of interpretation to extract a more edifying meaning from Greek myths, and this method had been taken over by Jewish writers in order to deal with the problems of the Old Testament. A few examples can be found in New Testament writers (e.g. Galatians 4:21-31), and it became a common Christian practice in the second century. In later times elaborate systems of interpretation were based on it. Some held that the Bible contained three levels of meaning: the literal, the moral

133

and the spiritual; sometimes additional levels were distinguished. In one form or another allegory remained the standard method of interpretation throughout the Middle Ages, and although at the Reformation the Protestant churches officially repudiated it, it may still be encountered. The obvious objection to it is that the 'hidden' meaning which we claim to draw out of Scripture can too easily be an alien idea which we are reading into it. The variety of allegorical interpretations of the same passage discredits the method itself. The point however is that allegorical interpretation was needed. It was by this means that the church coped with the difficulties and obscurities of an ancient book, and modern critical study has replaced it largely because it has been able to explain those problematical features more adequately.

Secondly, there were good historical reasons why critical study of the New Testament began when it did. It was part of a wider development. All departments of knowledge have grown in the last four hundred years. Many of the scholarly and scientific disciplines upon which our civilization is based are very recent in origin, and even the most ancient have been so radically revised that the medieval counterpart of a modern mathematician or doctor would hardly recognize his successor. With this growth of knowledge and new techniques it would have been surprising if there had not also been developments in biblical study.

The driving force in this movement was without doubt supplied by the questioning frame of mind. Curiosity and obstinate refusal to be put off with conventional half-answers have inspired biblical scholars as much as Newton, Darwin or Einstein. It was helped by three factors:

(a) The first was the effect of new discoveries and the consequent widening of horizons. It is not accidental that some of the earliest work was done on questions of the text, for it was in this field that the earliest discoveries were made, as long-forgotten manuscripts came to light in remote libraries. Archaeological discoveries similarly played a crucial role. As the ancient world was systematically uncovered, knowledge of its history, languages and everyday life were immeasurably increased.

(b) The second factor was the growth of scientific knowledge and with it of the scientific outlook which prompted the questions. Some difficulties about the creation stories had been felt even in the second century, but with the development of geology and biology in the nineteenth century the questions multiplied. In relation to the New Testament it was inevitable that questions should be asked, for example about miracles and belief in evil spirits. When the attempt was being made to bring everything in the universe within the compass of scientific study and explanation, the world of the Bible had to be included, if it was still to be regarded as part of the real world. In the popular mind this questioning is often associated with the effects in the late nineteenth century of Charles Darwin's work on evolution and natural selection, but Strauss had written twenty-five years earlier when the questions were already well aired. In fact the foundation for it was laid in the early eighteenth century through the work of the English deists, who insisted that reason must be applied to the Bible as to everything else and that no revealed truth could do violence to reason.

(c) The third factor was the development of historical perspective. We are now much more aware than was possible in earlier times of the ways in which historical periods differ from each other, not only in events but particularly in outlook, and of the dangers of reading back into the past ideas which are obvious to us but were unheard of at that time. The result was that the New Testament came to be seen as the product of a particular age, intelligible only by reference to its historical context.

Thus biblical scholarship must be seen as the product of its age; but this is not to imply that it is now superfluous. Before its rise the church was able to do without it only because it made use of a substitute.

(2) A second objection arises from the fact that on occasions scholars affirm as unassailable certainties views which only a few years later are radically revised. The layman easily concludes that scholarship is merely a matter of passing from one fashionable stopping-place to another. There is no need for him to venture into such exotic country; traditional views, like home, are best, and the erring scholar will eventually bring himself back to them.

We have seen evidence in our historical review to support this attitude. Long-settled issues tend to be reopened, and many new theories turn out to be the revival of old ones in a new guise.

135

For example the view advocated by S. G. F. Brandon in 1967, that Jesus was really a kind of zealot who sanctioned armed revolt against the Romans, is really only another form of the theory of Reimarus. Some recent work on the synoptic problem, which has attempted to overthrow the view we advocated in chapter 5, has done so by reverting to the theory first put forward by Griesbach in 1776, that Luke was based on Matthew, and Mark on both. More recently still (as we have already mentioned) J. A. T. Robinson has argued that all the New Testament documents should be dated before AD 70, a view very close to popular ideas; but, as he himself insists, he builds up his case by employing critical methods and not by ignoring them.

We have also seen that the history of scholarship is marked by the dominance of various fashions lasting usually only one or two decades. We have noted some of the schools which have held the field at certain times. In part their existence can be explained by the personal influence in the classroom and in publications of outstanding scholars. Such schools emerge partly because a new hypothesis is propounded or new discoveries are made, and in exploring their implications people are carried away by enthusiasm and only later recognize their limitations.

However, to regard the revival of old theories or the temporary ascendancy of particular schools of thought as a reason for rejecting the whole enterprise merely betrays a misunderstanding of the nature of the biblical scholar's work and the methods by which he reaches his conclusions.

The scholar has before him a certain quantity of evidence, much of it from the New Testament itself, but also from elsewhere. From this alone he has to deduce the answers to his questions. Unlike the scientist he cannot conduct any experiments to test his theories. The only tests available are adequacy and completeness: does the theory *fully* explain the evidence and does it explain *all* the evidence? If the evidence is incomplete or ambiguous, as is often the case, the decision has to be taken on the balance of probabilities. It can never be final.

Two considerations may lead him to change his mind. One, obviously, is the discovery of fresh evidence. We saw that discovery was a factor in the rise of critical study in the beginning. Every discovery of new material opens up fresh perspectives, and major discoveries have a far-reaching effect. The finding of

136

enormous quantities of papyrus documents in Egypt since 1890, for example, has not only helped the study of the New Testament text but led to a complete revision of ideas about its language, with the recognition that it was not a special 'sacred tongue', but the language of everyday life. The other development which will lead the scholar to change his views is simply that someone proposes a more adequate theory. The reputation of many of the greatest and most controversial figures in the history of scholarship rests on their ability to do this, and by so doing upset all previously held positions.

What, above all, the objection fails to recognize is that it is precisely by the reconsideration of established positions that all knowledge advances, in the arts and sciences generally as much as in biblical studies. It is in the nature of man to ask questions, and upon it his progress has always depended. In the history of New Testament scholarship one of the striking features is the number of really fundamental questions which were asked very early, by Reimarus, Strauss, Baur and others, to which scholars find themselves continually returning. But no definitive answer can be given to any question once and for all. Understanding always involves relating what we are studying to other aspects of our experience, and as the world never stands still, experience and ideas change, and so new questions arise and old ones have to be asked from a fresh standpoint. In every generation we face the task of understanding the New Testament for ourselves. Only in a completely static universe could it be otherwise, and those who complain that experts do not always agree or expect them never to change their minds are really asking that they cease to function.

In spite of this, as we have noted, progress is made. An enormous amount of detailed work has been done in the accumulation of the facts upon which theories are based, and this will not need to be repeated, although each scholar taking up the study of the subject will need to master it. Further, while final answers may be unattainable, it is certain that many wrong answers have been exposed and put away. An important illustration of this is the extent to which biblical scholarship has helped the churches to overcome denominational differences by providing insights into the meaning of the Bible which could be accepted on all sides as common ground. There is certainly no question of scholars one day returning full circle to the opinions of the common man in biblical studies any more than in medicine or astronomy.

(3) What protection, then, do we have against the prejudices with which a scholar comes to his work? We saw in our discussion of the Jesus of history that it is impossible for the historian to eliminate his own bias entirely, and examples can be given from the history of scholarship of the influence of Hegel's philosophy on F. C. Baur, or of the existentialism of Martin Heidegger on Bultmann.

In practice most scholars try to be as impartial as they can and seek the truth, however unpalatable. Of course there are always a few campaigners whose primary interest in scholarship is to use its results to advocate some cause to which they are dedicated, but scholarship must not be judged by those who manipulate it. Nevertheless we have to admit that every scholar is biased. In part it is a matter of temperament: some are more conservatively inclined than others. It has been well said that scholars can be divided into those who by nature doubt everything until it has been proved true, and those who accept everything until it has been proved false. In part however the bias of the scholar is simply the evidence that he is human. Every person is influenced, not only by his own prejudices but by the prejudices of the age in which he lives, of which he and his contemporaries may be largely unaware and unable to correct. Only later ages can correct them – from a new standpoint, but never from a position free from all prejudice. This is true of scholars of all persuasions; it is equally true of the conservative critic of all scholarship. It is one of the limitations of human knowledge.

When that has been said there are practical correctives to prejudice. There are always the facts, which have to be accounted for. There are the tests of completeness and adequacy to which we have referred. There is the questioning mind which refuses to be satisfied with answers given so far. Above all there is the scholarly community. Every scholar's theories have to be submitted to the judgement of his informed colleagues in many countries, who share his breadth of knowledge. While twenty men and women can be as mistaken as one, it is generally worthwhile to pay more attention to the consensus of scholarly opinion than to the views of an individual.

It might help, of course, if scholars were less given to dogmatism. If they more frequently hedged their statements about with qualifications, so reminding their audiences of the provisional nature of their work, they might save some from feeling let down by a dramatic change of view, and they would certainly frustrate others who mistakenly look for cut and dried answers.

Dogmatic pronouncements however are not confined to scholars. They are just as often heard from the opponents of scholarship, with less justification. The scholar has at least one advantage. A lifetime's study of his subject will have given him a familiarity with the ancient world, and a consequent ability to detect and interpret clues in the New Testament, which other readers would miss. His experience is analogous to that which enables the consultant physician to make accurate diagnoses which only investigative surgery could confirm or disprove. The New Testament expert lacks that possibility of proof, but his knowledge deserves the same respect, even though (in both fields) experts can sometimes be shown to be wrong. But in the interpretation of the Bible great issues are at stake, and it is not surprising that strong passions are aroused.

11. Authority and Meaning

One of the most important facts to emerge from our study of the New Testament has been that it must be seen in three-dimensional terms. It has depth as well as surface. It is the product of over a century of church life, and behind its pages stands a living community in all its variety. The writings which it comprises were composed at different dates and reflect different, even conflicting points of view. Within the same document earlier writings and oral traditions may be taken over and adapted to new purposes; the same words may be invested with new levels of meaning. Particularly is this the case with the teaching of Jesus, where we have to reckon with a series of adaptations both in oral tradition and at the stage when the gospels were written.

This point can be illustrated if we turn back to the Lord's Prayer, with which we began this study in chapter 1. We saw then that many of the differences between the English versions were due to problems of translation, or could be traced back to variant readings in early manuscripts which were unknown to the translators of 1611, whose versions in Matthew and Luke were consequently much closer to each other than those of 1961. But not all the differences could be explained in that way, and we can now go further, making use of the approaches to the gospels which we have described in previous chapters.

The close similarity in wording of many clauses of the prayer suggests that Matthew's and Luke's versions go back to a common Greek original, which has subsequently undergone modification before being reproduced in the two gospels. Whether the modifications were introduced in the course of oral tradition or by the evangelists themselves is more difficult to determine. Certainly some of the differences are characteristic of the evangelists. Matthew much more frequently refers to God as being *in heaven* (cf. above, page 6, line 2) than Mark or Luke, while Luke's particular expression in line 7, *each day*, is very

140

similar to one he has inserted (at 9:23) into material taken from Mark, and is therefore very likely to be a contribution of his own. Probably the prayer was modified both by the evangelists and by oral tradition before them.

It is generally agreed, however, that the Greek original was itself a translation of an Aramaic prayer. A recent writer on the prayer, J. Jeremias argues that Luke preserves the original brevity of the prayer, while Matthew has remained more faithful to its original wording, so that the earliest form should be translated:

Dear Father,*
Hallowed be thy name,
Thy Kingdom come,
Our bread for tomorrow
    give us today,
And forgive us our debts
    as we herewith forgive our debtors,
And let us not succumb to the trial.

(*An attempt to reproduce in English the familiar tone of the one Aramaic word, *Abba*.)

What evidence is there that such a prayer actually goes back to Jesus? Although there is no one Jewish prayer which provides a parallel for everything, there are many parallels to individual clauses in other Jewish prayers, and this might be thought (by the criterion of dissimilarity, see above, page 117) to point to an origin in the Jewish Christian church. But the simple address, *Father* (as in Luke) is unique to the prayers of Jesus, and by the same criterion is likely to be original; so also is the way in which the prayer for forgiveness is linked to the petitioner's willingness to forgive.

If the prayer as reconstructed does derive from Jesus, what meaning did it have? In Jeremias' view the key is to be found in the double emphasis of the message of Jesus. On the one hand the kingdom of God is soon to come; on the other those who respond to Jesus' call may here and now experience the benefits which the kingdom will bring. Thus the prayer shows that his disciples can share in the intimate knowledge of God which was Jesus' privilege, and call him Father; they can ask to receive

141

today the 'bread', both material and spiritual sustenance, which properly belongs to the great 'tomorrow' when the kingdom will come; they can experience now the forgiveness which is God's prerogative at the Last Judgement. At the same time they still look forward to the kingdom and pray for its coming in the future, when God will make all men acknowledge that he is God (*hallowed be thy name*). The coming of the kingdom will however be a time of testing when many will be tempted to turn away from God, and the prayer ends with a plea to be preserved from this.

But if this analysis of its meaning in the teaching of Jesus is correct, it is clear that for the authors of the gospels the prayer did not have quite this meaning. For both of them the petition *Thy Kingdom come* is robbed of some of its intensity by the conviction, evident elsewhere in their writings, that there may nevertheless be some delay in its arrival (cf. for example Luke 17:20f., Acts 1:7f., Matthew 24:3-6). Luke (in line 7) sees the prayer as a request for daily sustenance in the continuing life of discipleship, to match the daily carrying of the cross (9:23). In any case the situation has changed since the time of Jesus. His death for sinners and his resurrection have given a new meaning both to the request to be forgiven and to the prayer for deliverance.

We can therefore trace at least four versions of the Lord's Prayer from the evidence provided by the New Testament, and for each of these there is a new emphasis or perspective which affects the meaning even of those words which are unchanged.

We can take this observation a stage further. So far as we can trace, the Lord's Prayer has always been a prayer Christians have said together. In consequence it has taken on a life of its own. Apart from the variant forms which manuscript readings illustrate, the old words have acquired new meanings. Whatever *daily bread* meant for Jesus, it is certain that for generations of Christians in its setting in the Communion Service it has meant primarily the Body of Christ in the consecrated bread.

Two questions arise from these observations, and this chapter is devoted to a brief discussion of them. The first concerns the authority and inspiration of the New Testament.

The New Testament scholar is, rightly, never allowed to forget for long that the collection of writings he studies enjoys

142

unique authority in the church. As we saw in chapter 3, the question of authority was fundamental to the gathering of the collection at the outset, and its preservation over the centuries is entirely due to its status as sacred Scripture. Often the work of scholars has been opposed on the grounds that they were undermining this authority. In the past, for example, attempts to publish a more accurate Greek text have been resisted as attacks on the Word of God. Today the issues which cause most concern along these lines are pseudepigraphy and the historical reliability of the gospels and Acts. It is not uncommon to find more conservative scholars arguing that, because the books concerned have been acknowledged by the church as being within the Canon, they must be the authentic productions of the authors to whom they are attributed, and that if they appear to give historical information they must actually do so.

The question which has to be faced, however, is where we should begin. Are we to start from preconceived ideas of what the authority and inspiration of the Bible mean, and deduce from them what sort of document the Bible must be, refusing to admit any evidence from within the Bible or elsewhere which appears to conflict with it; or should we begin by looking carefully at the Bible as we have it, and working out from that how its authority and inspiration are to be understood? It has been the contention of this book throughout that the latter is the only procedure to be followed with integrity. There is no need to deny either the authority of the New Testament or its inspiration, but we are required to reconsider what we mean by these terms. Thus, as we saw in our discussion of pseudepigraphy in chapter 4, what matters primarily is the author's intention. We must not impose on any biblical author aims which he did not have, however appropriate we may think them to be.

A similar response must be made to the problem concerning authority which has now come before us. An aspect of the church's recognition of the authority of the New Testament was the (often unspoken) assumption that Scripture is unanimous. The Bible, in both Testaments, was held to speak with one voice, and any part could be quoted equally. As early as the second century the question was raised whether the Old Testament could be regarded in the same light as the New, but on the whole the unitary view prevailed. But in the light of what we have seen about the New Testament this assumption must be reconsidered. There is conflict as well as agreement within its pages. The same passage may preserve several levels of meaning. Which is to be taken as authoritative? For the letters of Paul, the Acts of the Apostles or the book of Revelation it would seem obvious that the authority should lie in the author's meaning rather than in his sources, but what then of the gospels? Do we disregard the original meaning of the teaching of Jesus in preference for Matthew's (or John's) understanding of it? If, on the other hand, we allow that in the gospels the authority lies in their ultimate source, does this imply a similar decision for passages in the epistles which preserve traditional material? Again, if we hold that Paul in his letters carries authority, can we have the same attitude to the letters to Timothy and Titus, if we accept that they were not written by Paul and at points conflict with his teaching?

A partial solution to these problems is offered by those who advocate a revision of the Canon in order to eliminate disputed books. I have argued against this in chapter 3 (page 35). In any case it does not deal with the problem of different levels of meaning within the same text. A different solution, popular some years ago, was to argue that Jesus himself is the Word of God, and that all New Testament teaching should be assessed by reference to him. Hence the authority of the various parts was made relative to one central authority. The attraction of this approach lies in its apparent basis in John 1:14, and in the fact that when the Canon was formed it was the Lord's authority which it was held to represent. Recent work on the Jesus of history however has emphasized the difficulty of the view. It is impossible completely to separate Jesus from the church's witness to him, so as to set him over against it as a norm in the way we require. To complete the reference to John 1:14, our access to the Word made flesh is through the witness of those who beheld his glory.

The only other alternative is to accept the Canon as it stands and face the consequences squarely. Because the New Testament does not speak with one voice, we cannot expect to quote it as the authoritative answer to all our present-day problems. If the early church embraced different viewpoints, we must either allow the same freedom today, or find some way of showing theological reasons for preferring one to another. The New Testament is not an oracle but a witness to God.

A similar conclusion may be reached about inspiration. It has been understood in various ways. In the early centuries it was often thought of as a form of possession, God speaking directly through the writer whose natural powers were suspended, in much the same way as a spirit is thought to communicate through a medium. A less mechanical explanation was that the Holy Spirit suggested the ideas to the writer, who then expressed them in his own words. This allowed for differences of style between authors. In effect both views saw God as the author and the human writers as no more than mouthpieces, or at best secretaries.

If one begins from such a view of inspiration one is driven to conclude that the Bible must be infallible and without inner contradiction of any kind. Any form of critical questioning, however mild, must be seen as an attempt to interrogate God. But, as with authority, it is vital to ask whether this is necessarily the only understanding of inspiration. If we begin from the New Testament as we have it we may conclude that a better analogy is to be found in preaching. As every preacher knows, no sermon is infallible; he may at a later date revise much or all of it. Yet his hearers may be conscious, on both earlier and later occasions on which it is preached, that the preacher's own faith has been communicated to them in such a way that they have made it their own. Through his words God has spoken. This is a better analogy because the New Testament, like the Old, is the product of faith; deliberately or incidentally its writers bear witness to what they believe, and through their writings their faith is still transmitted to us; God speaks. But this does not entail their infallibility. To say that the New Testament is inspired is only to say that God speaks to us through it. If we go on to claim that it is uniquely inspired (and therefore in a different category from last Sunday's sermon), we are not describing the manner in which it is inspired, but pointing out that, unlike the sermon, it has canonical authority.

Thus our understanding of New Testament authority and inspiration must start from a recognition of what the New Testament is. The theologian can no longer use it as a collection of proof-texts, simply taking sentences in isolation and quoting

145

them out of context to reinforce doctrines. One text does not necessarily speak for the whole. The context of a statement, the circumstances in which it is made, the possibility that it is only one view among many – all these must be taken into account. Theologians generally recognize this in principle, but it cannot be said that they always observe it in practice.

We turn now to the other question which arises from our opening discussion of levels within the New Testament. It concerns what we may call continuity of meaning. If the Lord's Prayer, or a parable like that of the bailiff (see above, page 77) has undergone a series of adaptations to new situations in which the same words have acquired new or modified meanings, what is the connexion between them? How do we determine whether an adaptation is justified?

The problem forced itself upon the New Testament church. 'Not everyone who calls me "Lord, Lord" will enter the kingdom of Heaven, but only those who do the will of my heavenly Father' (Matthew 7:21) is a warning that in some circumstances the repetition of words may be illegitimate, for in the new context, without obedience, they have lost their original meaning as a confession of loyalty. But the problem arose particularly in relation to the Old Testament, for Christians found themselves at variance with Jews in their interpretation of the Old Testament as referring to Christ (cf. above, page 91).

The relationship between Christian belief and the Old Testament could be expressed in various ways. A promise made by God to the fathers or a prophetic declaration of what he will one day accomplish was seen to be fulfilled in the events involving Jesus (for example Galatians 3:8, Romans 15:12). Besides explicit prophecies other sentences might be taken as prophetic in a similar way (Romans 8:36). A broader relationship was suggested by the approach known today as typology, by which the Old Testament was seen to suggest patterns in God's dealings with the world to which he had again conformed in sending Christ, and which therefore illuminated Christ's coming. The flood, the exodus, and (more by contrast) the fall of Adam could be seen in this way (I Peter 3:19-21; I Corinthians 5:7f.; Romans 5:12-21). On occasions as we have seen (see above, page 133), allegory could be used; but it must be emphasized that it was not just contemporary experiences in some general sense which were

146

felt to be the fulfilment of the Old Testament, but specifically the new situation brought about by Christ. The problem with all these approaches however was the same: what is it about the present situation which justifies the claim that in it the ancient promise is fulfilled? It is not too wide of the mark to sum up the Jewish-Christian debate in the early church by saying that for the church the resurrection of Jesus was the justification for claiming that he fulfilled Scripture, while for the Jews his crucifixion proved that he did not.

Today we see the same problem of continuity within the New Testament itself. One aspect of it is the problem raised in chapter 9 about the connexion between the Jesus of history and the Lord proclaimed by the church; another, the relationship between levels of meaning with which we began. But in reality the problem is much wider, for it concerns our understanding of the New Testament today. The Lord's Prayer is in some respects in a special category in being taken over as a Christian prayer, but it illustrates a more general problem. As it has been read and expounded in worship over the centuries, the New Testament has been heard with new meanings. It has become the expression of the church's faith as much as its source, taking on new significance in changing historical circumstances and different cultures. What links all these meanings together? How does one distinguish a legitimate interpretation from the arbitrary misuse of ancient words to express something quite different?

We introduced these questions in chapter 1, when we discussed the difficulties of interpreting an ancient text. The traditional answer to them is that the key to the New Testament is provided by the tradition of the church, which has accumulated a body of insight into its meaning and application. This is the formal position of the Roman Catholic Church, but most Christian denominations also have their traditional ways of understanding the Bible, which influence interpretation in practice although there is no dogmatic recognition of the authority of tradition. It is not a fully satisfactory answer however, because there come moments in history when, on the basis of the text, people are led to challenge the faithfulness of the traditional interpretation.

The historical approach to the Bible has underlined the difficulty. Where the Bible is not acknowledged to be an ancient book, the danger is always that it will be read as though it were

147

contemporary, meanings being injected into its words which they could not possibly have carried. Allegorical interpretation is one form of this, although many modern readers do it unconsciously without allegorizing. But once the distance between our world and the world of the Bible has been recognized, there is no escaping the problem. The reader may attempt to resist what we have called the adaptation of the meaning of the Bible to the modern world, by trying to turn his back on his own culture and deliberately adopting the language and ideas of the ancient world. Whether the attempt is theologically justifiable is open to debate, but it is certain that it cannot really be successful. No one can seriously adopt an ancient outlook on life in every respect, and there must be in consequence many points at which modern ideas are unconsciously introduced, with the added danger that they are claimed to have the authority of being 'biblical'.

The discussion of these problems has become a central interest of New Testament scholars in recent years, under the heading of *hermeneutics*. Originally this term meant simply the study of the rules which were to be applied in interpreting Scripture, but today it is used in a broader sense, to cover the more basic question how we may understand the meaning of an ancient writing at all. The debate, though sometimes irritatingly technical, is to be welcomed, for biblical scholars have not always recognized the importance of the question. Too often in the past they have assumed that their task was complete when they had set out the meaning of the biblical text in its original setting. This is doubtless the reason why so many ordinary readers have felt modern commentaries and books on the New Testament to be unsatisfactory. The discussion of hermeneutics implies the recognition that this is not enough. It is not only that the New Testament is still used within the church, and the present significance is as important as the original historical meaning; it is that in the last resort the two aspects cannot be kept apart. Any attempt to state what an ancient author meant which goes beyond merely repeating his own words is a step in the direction of saying what he means now, for it involves using modern terminology. The danger is therefore always present that what we see of his meaning will depend on what makes sense to us now.

148

Eschatology, a term which does not occur in the New Testament but abounds in textbooks, provides a good illustration. In many parts of the New Testament the confidence is expressed that the kingdom of God, or the Son of Man, or Christ, will come soon, within the lifetime of writer and readers, with the implication that the present world-order will then be superseded by another. In that form at least the hope has remained unfulfilled. There are several ways in which the interpreter may deal with such passages. He may emphasize their literal meaning, and perhaps go on implicitly to discredit those who held such hopes. Alternatively he may argue that the imminent aspect of the hope was not essential to it; a promise was being affirmed, but it was merely assumed that it would be fulfilled soon. He may go further and argue that the essence of the hope did not lie in the temporal aspect at all, but in certain basic, timeless convictions about God and his power to save: God is always near, and believers must always be ready for him. The interpreter will of course look for clues in the relevant passages to justify the interpretation he has chosen, but there is no denying that some interpretations are also much easier to accommodate to the twentieth century; indeed the interpretation is itself the beginning of such an accommodation, for the language it employs is not the language used in the passages themselves.

The hermeneutical debate therefore tends to be concerned with the extent to which the two stages, historical interpretation and contemporary adaptation, can be kept apart: how the interpreter can protect himself from merely seeing in the New Testament what he wants to see, and how he can best equip himself to distil the essence from its pages. A term often used in this connexion is *pre-understanding*, that is the understanding one must already have of a subject if one is to make sense of any literature about it. A reader of this book who has never seen a New Testament will have little idea of what we have been discussing. A preliminary acquaintance of this kind is essential, whatever the subject – music, mathematics, art, or religion – for it determines the questions one asks in one's mind when reading. Further, one can approach a book from different points of view which may or may not coincide with what the author hoped for. Today one is likely to read a sixteenth-century book on medicine, not to learn about medicine but about the ideas of the sixteenth century or about the history of the development of medical knowledge. One may read the New Testament from a similar point of view, as an example of great literature, or as a source for the history of religions; but what is the correct approach? What 'pre-understanding' is necessary if we are to interpret it rightly?

One theological tradition, following the lead of Karl Barth, insists that the Bible in this respect is an exception. There can be no pre-understanding, for unredeemed man can have no prior knowledge of the subject of the Bible, God, who creates knowledge of himself only by speaking to man. Scholars in the existentialist tradition, on the other hand, notably R. Bultmann, have argued that it is our basic experience of being human, human existence as existentialist thought analyses it, which provides the necessary key. To this condition the Bible speaks, for this is what we have in common with its authors.

It is Bultmann in fact who has done more than most to impress these questions on the general public, by proposing a programme for 'demythologizing' the New Testament. The New Testament, he insists, is mythological throughout. On every page it assumes an outlook on the world with which modern man cannot identify himself: a three-decker universe, with heaven above and hell beneath, which had a beginning in time only a few thousand years ago and will come to an end shortly, and is populated by demons and angels. No modern man in a scientific age can seriously believe all this. Yet there is a genuine gospel in its pages: a call to decision for God and for living in absolute trust in him. The centre of this gospel is the cross of Jesus. Originally the mythological elements helped to convey the gospel; now they hinder it. If people are to hear it today it must be expressed in contemporary terms, set free from its mythological prison. Existentialism provides for Bultmann the contemporary language and with its aid he interprets Jesus, Paul and John. This is not subordinating the gospel to an alien philosophy, in the way that scholars have done in the past, for in Bultmann's view existentialism is not alien; it offers a key which fits.

Not all would accept this position. One criticism of Bultmann is that he makes the message of the New Testament man-centred rather than God-centred. There is certainly a danger that the 'pre-understanding' we bring to the New Testament will restrict

150

our vision, and prevent us from recognizing what the text is saying. On the basis of this, advocates of what has come to be known as the 'new hermeneutic' (E. Fuchs and G. Ebeling among them) have stressed the importance of the text itself as calling our presuppositions in question, rather than (with Bultmann) our attempted reconstruction of the author's understanding of existence lying behind it, which may be no more than a mirror of our own prejudices from which we need to be liberated. However, they give the impression that they regard what the text actually says to the reader, regardless of the author's intentions, as decisive, and if this is so, they would seem to be taking a step backward to a pre-critical age.

None of these replies is fully satisfactory. Certainly no simple rule of thumb can be offered which will assure us that we have interpreted the inner meaning of a given passage correctly. What the debate about hermeneutics does stress, however, is the necessity for constant self-examination on the part of the interpreter, so that he may be as aware as possible of the presuppositions of his own approach, and be ready to correct them when he finds that they do not coincide with the presuppositions of the writer he is studying.

The ordinary reader of the Bible is not of course usually so sophisticated. He may read it for a variety of motives. Parts of it may 'ring bells' with him for different reasons. But the quest for a *true* understanding is important to anyone who considers the Bible itself to be important. As we saw in our study of Jesus, it is impossible to have a neutral, 'objective' interpretation of any part of the New Testament. The insights of the student whose own religious commitment (if any) lies elsewhere can sometimes be illuminating, but since the New Testament is the product of men of Christian faith, in the last resort there can be no full penetration into its meaning without at least the readiness to share their faith.

Conclusion

We have pleaded in this book that the New Testament be recognized for what it is: a collection of ancient documents, preserving a variety of viewpoints and levels of meaning within an overall unity of faith in the risen Jesus of Nazareth, and carrying authority for the Christian church. In chapter 11 we indicated briefly how this affected our understanding of its inspiration and authority, and suggested the consequences for its use in theology.

Professional theologians, however, account for only a small proportion of those who use the New Testament, and we conclude by considering the wider implications of our review of scholarship for other users.

Worship remains, as always in the past, the primary context in which the Bible is used. This use is not confined to the lessons and sermon. Many individual sentences, like the Lord's Prayer as a whole, have taken on new life as expressions of devotion. The words of the centurion in Matthew 8:8, for example, are often used, with slight adaptation, in preparation for Communion. It is right that this should be so. The power of all great literature resides in its ability to provide images and symbols which influence the mind and emotions. Many quotations from the Bible have become almost proverbial in this way, with a meaning quite unrelated to their original context. Their meaning is given by the context in which they are now used.

Yet if the words are felt to be more than proverbial, if they are still used partly because they are biblical, and are intended to remind us of their original context and its associations (as is surely the case for example with the Lord's Prayer or the canticles, the *Magnificat* and *Nunc Dimittis*), then the questions about continuity of meaning raised in chapter 11 apply. In what way is a Christian congregation today in a situation analogous to that of Mary in Luke 1:46ff., and how far can her words be adapted without destroying their original sense? This is not a

152

simple question about the adaptation of ancient writings; it concerns the continuity and identity of the church and its faith through centuries of change.

In preaching, the situation is slightly different. If it is related to the reading of the Bible at all, whether by the announcement of a text or by taking up the themes of the lessons, the sermon is explicitly functioning as a bridge between the ancient Scriptures and the contemporary situation. The preacher is confronted with the problems of continuity of meaning.

Unfortunately this is often not recognized, chiefly because the antiquity of the Bible and the gap between past and present are not acknowledged. A text is announced at the beginning and used as a slogan or motto for the sermon without regard for its original meaning. How many essays in banal optimism have been based on the (almost certainly incorrect) Authorized Version rendering of Romans 8:28, 'all things work together for good to them that love God'! This proceeding is dishonest. If a biblical text is used in a sermon, the intention, however unconscious, is to 'borrow' the authority of the Bible for what follows, the impression being given that the one supports the other. In that case it is dishonest not to do justice to the meaning of the text. The preacher has a responsibility to discover, so far as he can, what the writer on whose prestige he is leaning intended to say, and to represent that meaning to the best of his ability, although not of course to confine his remarks to the historical sense.

A particular application of our plea for preachers to acknowledge the New Testament for what it is concerns the gospels. Far too many sermons still treat them as verbatim records of events, and indulge in speculations about the motives and inner thoughts of the characters involved which are illegitimate in the light of what we now know the gospels to be. How can we know what Jesus was thinking when he called the Twelve, still less what was going on in the mind of the devil at the temptations? We do not have the evidence to recreate events in this way, and usually such efforts only miss the point which the narrative is trying to make. Often, too, preachers harmonize selected portions of all the gospels to produce a composite narrative which rides roughshod over the intention of each gospel and the meaning of the excerpts in their own contexts. The way in which the 'seven words from the cross' are treated in Good Friday sermons is a case in point. Too little attention is given by preachers to the contribution of redaction criticism in elucidating the needs in the church which a given passage in the gospels is designed to meet.

Preachers are members of a wider group of users of the New Testament who, in the present situation, are becoming increasingly important, and may be called the 'middle-men'. With the fast-expanding frontiers of knowledge and the growing specialization of scholars in ever more limited fields, there is increased need for those who will ensure that the results of scholarship are communicated widely to people in the churches and to the public generally. There are distressing signs of a wide gap between the views of scholars and those of ordinary people. In the extent of his technical knowledge the biblical scholar must always be ahead of others, but this should not be the case in respect of his basic attitude. There is fault on both sides, but the malaise will be cured only if the work of scholars is properly communicated and interpreted by those who are in a position to do so. In this respect the role of teachers in schools is vitally important, both in the dissemination of knowledge and in encouraging the right attitude. It is tragic that so many people retain, or imagine they are expected to retain an attitude to the Bible which was made obsolete a hundred years ago, and it is not surprising that at some time they reject a Bible which they have regarded in this way. The seeds of these attitudes are sown in day school and Sunday school, and it is here above all that reform must begin. The alternative to such over-literal attitudes, and to the equally false, negative approach which seeks merely to debunk it, is to recognize the New Testament for what it is.

Not all those who study the New Testament in an educational setting will themselves be adherents of the Christian faith, although they will fail to understand it unless they recognize its importance for Christians. For many ordinary believers however its chief use is in daily devotions. Has modern scholarship made it a closed book, replacing the priesthood of the Middle Ages, who alone were able to read the Latin text, by a new priesthood of biblical experts who now hold the key to its secrets? In part the words of the New Testament have always had an immediate impact, and this has not been diminished.

In part it has always been obscure and has required an interpreter. In the last two centuries the biblical scholar has joined the theologian and the preacher, who have traditionally exercised this function, not to replace but to assist them. Of course, many fond illusions about the New Testament have been shattered in the process, but on the positive side we now understand much more than ever about its meaning in its original setting and the possibilities of its message for today. In particular it is now easier to recognize that a living Christian community stands behind its pages. Modern scholarship has brought out the individuality of those who contributed to its composition, showing them as real human beings, wrestling with the problems of life in the church and the world, striving to hold on to, and to interpret their faith in changing circumstances. It is easier to feel an affinity with these men and women, and to learn from them the meaning of Christian faith.

The individual reader therefore need not feel inhibited about reading the New Testament, but it is doubtful if he should attempt to read it on its own. He should draw on the help of commentaries and dictionaries, read generally about its background and contents, and so try to reach its meaning. The New Testament has been preserved by the church over the centuries because it is felt that its ancient words still speak, and in order that they should continue to speak. The purpose of its existence is fulfilled only when, in the context of Christian faith, it is read reflectively and applied to life. So far from inhibiting this, modern scholarship makes the New Testament come alive.

Further Reading

The literature on the New Testament is very extensive. This is a short selection of books which will take the reader a step further on the topics discussed in each chapter. The English publication date is usually quoted for foreign works.

General

R. A. Spivey and D. M. Smith Jr., *Anatomy of the New Testament: A Guide to its Structure and Meaning*, Collier-MacMillan, 2nd edition, 1974.

C. F. D. Moule, *The Birth of the New Testament*, A. and C. Black, 2nd edition, 1966.

R. M. Grant, *Historical Introduction to the New Testament*, Fontana, 1971.

In addition there are many excellent articles in

G. A. Buttrick and others (ed.), *The Interpreter's Dictionary of the Bible*, Nelson, 1962.

Chapter 1

J. Jeremias, *The Lord's Prayer in the Light of Recent Research*, to be found in Batey, *New Testament Issues,* SCM Press, 1970, and in Jeremias, *The Prayers of Jesus*, SCM Press, 1967.

C. F. Evans, *The Lord's Prayer*, S.P.C.K., 1963.

H. F. D. Sparks, *On Translations of the Bible*, Athlone Press, 1973.

R. M. Grant – as above.

Chapter 2

It is impossible to make a full study of textual criticism without a knowledge of Greek, but a good introduction is given in

B. M. Metzger, *The Text of the New Testament*, O.U.P., 1964.

Chapter 3

In addition to the books listed under chapter 4 see

K. Aland, *The Problem of the New Testament Canon*, Mowbray, 1962.

Chapter 4

Introductions to the literature of the New Testament vary in the amount of detail they give and in the relatively 'radical' or 'conservative' positions they adopt. A sample of this variety may be seen in the following:

R. H. Fuller, *A Critical Introduction to the New Testament*, Duckworth, 1971.

D. Guthrie, *New Testament Introduction*, I.V.P., 3rd edition 1970.

W. G. Kümmel, *Introduction to the New Testament*, SCM Press, 2nd edition 1975.

W. Marxsen, *Introduction to the New Testament*, SCM Press, 1968.

J. A. T. Robinson, *Redating the New Testament*, SCM Press, 1976.

On both pseudepigraphy and the use of computers see

K. Aland and others, *The Authorship and Integrity of the New Testament*, S.P.C.K., 1965.

Chapter 5

V. Taylor, *The Gospels: A Short Introduction*, Epworth Press, 7th edition 1952.

The classic statement is

B. H. Streeter, *The Four Gospels*, MacMillan, 1924.

Its leading critic is

W. R. Farmer, *The Synoptic Problem*, Collier-MacMillan, 1964.

Chapter 6

V. Taylor, *The Formation of the Gospel Tradition*, MacMillan, 2nd edition 1935.

A more detailed treatment is to be found in

R. Bultmann, *History of the Synoptic Tradition*, 1921 (Eng. trans. Blackwell, 1963).

Special aspects are discussed in

J. Jeremias, *The Parables of Jesus*, SCM Press, 2nd edition 1963, and in the first chapter of

H. Riesenfeld, *The Gospel Tradition*, Mowbray, 1971.

Chapter 7

R. E. Brown, *The Gospel According to John* (especially the Introduction), Chapman, 1966.

B. Lindars, *Behind the Fourth Gospel*, S.P.C.K., 1971.

C. H. Dodd, *The Apostolic Preaching and its Developments*, Hodder & Stoughton, 2nd edition 1944.

A. M. Hunter, *Paul and his Predecessors*, SCM Press, 2nd edition 1961.

C. K. Barrett, *Luke the Historian in Recent Study*, Epworth Press, 1961.

G. Bornkamm, *Paul*, Hodder & Stoughton, 1971.

Chapter 8

N. Perrin, *What is Redaction Criticism?*, S.P.C.K., 1970.

J. Rohde, *Rediscovering the Teaching of the Evangelists*, SCM Press, 1968.

Chapter 9

As one might expect, books on the life and teaching of Jesus, and on the question how much of either we can recover, are legion. A beginning may be made with the following:

H. K. McArthur, *In Search of the Historical Jesus*, S.P.C.K., 1970.

N. Perrin, *Rediscovering the Teaching of Jesus*, SCM Press, 1967.

J. Jeremias, *New Testament Theology*, vol. 1, *The Proclamation of Jesus*, SCM Press, 1971.

R. Bultmann, *Jesus and the Word*, Collins, 1958.

G. Bornkamm, *Jesus of Nazareth*, Hodder & Stoughton, 1960.

Chapter 10

An excellent history of scholarship is to be found in

S. C. Neill, *The Interpretation of the New Testament, 1861–1961*, O.U.P., 1966.

See also

W. G. Kümmel, *The New Testament: the History of the Investigation of its Problems*, SCM Press, 1973.

Chapter 11

For hermeneutics see

R. E. Brown's article (no. 71) in R. E. Brown, J. A. Fitzmeyer and R. E. Murphy (ed.), *The Jerome Biblical Commentary*, Chapman, 1968.

For demythologizing, see especially

R. Bultmann's opening article in H. W. Bartsch (ed.), *Kerygma and Myth*, vol. 1, S.P.C.K., 1953.

C. E. Braaten, *History and Hermeneutics*, Lutterworth Press, 1968.

For other aspects see

J. Barr, *The Bible in the Modern World*, SCM Press, 1973.

D. E. Nineham (ed.), *The Church's Use of the Bible*, S.P.C.K., 1963.

Index

161

Kingdom of God, *see* Eschatology

Kittel, G., 130f

Koine text, 23

L', 62, 66

Last day(s), *see* Eschatology

Lazarus, parable of rich man and, 76, 78f

Lectionaries, 19

Lessing, G. E., 125

Liberal Protestantism, 113f, 127, 129

Lightfoot, J. B., 126, 128

Loisy, A., 129

Lord's Prayer, 5–15, 22, 38, 121, 140–42, 146f, 152

'M', 62, 65f

Magnificat, 152

Manuscripts, 16–26

Marcion, 33

Mark's gospel – outline of, 108, 119; – priority of, 62–64

Meaning, 11–15, 137, 140–42, 146–51, 152f

Messiah, 81, 101; *see* Christology

Messianic secret, 129

Methods of scholarship, 50f, 116–23, 136–39

Minuscules, 18

Miracle stories, 69

Morton, A. Q., 51

Multiple attestation, criterion of, 118

Nag Hammadi, 132

New English Bible, 5, 9

New Hermeneutic, 151

New quest of the historical Jesus, 121, 132

Nunc Dimittis, 152

Old Testament – canon of, 27, 29f; – in the New, 29, 89–91, 96, 112f, 130, 143, 146f

Oral tradition, 22, 30f, 71–76, 85–94, 111

Origen, 26, 133

Palaeography, 19

Palestinian background, 117

Palestinian Jewish Christianity, 80

Papyrus, 17f, 137

Parables, 72, 77f, 119, 127f, 146

Parallelism, 70

Parchment, 18

Paul, 34, 85–87, 93f, 111; – and Jesus, 93; – letters of, 30, 41f

Pericopae, 69, 103, 106

Peter – gospel of, 34; – reminiscences of, 71f; second letter of, 28, 32f, 38–46, 50, 93

Polycarp, 28

Pontifical Biblical Commission, 129f

Preaching, 88f, 153

Pre-understanding, 149–51

Progress in scholarship, 135–38

Pronouncement stories, 69f

Prophecy, 96, 111f

Proto-Luke, 65f, 102

Pseudonymity (pseudepigraphy), 52–54, 143

'Q', 62–67

Quest of the historical Jesus, 114; *see* History

Qumran, 132

Rabbinic Judaism, 75f

Redaction criticism, 95–109, 129, 131, 154

Reimarus, H., 125, 127f, 136f

Reitzenstein, R., 129

Return of Christ, *see* Eschatology

Richardson, A., 130

Rich man and Lazarus, parable of, 76, 78f

Riesenfeld, H., 75, 157

Robinson, J. A. T., 48, 136, 157

Roman Catholic scholarship, 129, 132, 147

Sayings of Jesus, 70f, 73, 78f, 111, 119

Scholarship, history of, 124–32

'Schools' of scholars, 125–32, 136

Schweitzer, A., 128f

Scientific outlook, 134f

Secret, messianic, 129

Secretaries, 52f

Serapion of Antioch, 34

Sermons in Acts, 92

Simon, R., 124, 128

Sinaiticus, Codex, 18, 26

Sitz im Leben, 80, 88, 103

Stories about Christ, 71

Strack, H., 132

Strauss, D. F., 125, 130f, 135, 137

Streeter, B. H., 62–66, 68, 103, 157

Subjectivity in scholarship, 51, 105f, 121f

Supernatural, 122

Symbolism, 152

Synoptic gospels *and* synoptic problem, 57–67, 93, 95, 128, 136

Tatian, 104

Tendency, 107, 126

Testimonies, 90

Textual criticism, 8, 16–26, 100, 124–26, 128, 142f

Tischendorf, C., 18

Traditio-historical method, 1, 79

Tradition, 22, 68–94, 106–08, 147

Translation problems, 8–10

Trial of Jesus, 118

Tübingen school, 125f

Two-document hypothesis, 66

Typology, 146

Uncials, 18

Understanding, nature of, 137

Unity of New Testament, 25, 35f, 93, 130, 143

Vellum, 18

Versions, 19f

Vulgate, 23

Weiss, J., 127f

Westcott, B. F., 126, 128

Wettstein, J. J., 125

Worship, 22, 31f, 34f, 89, 142, 152

Wolfenbüttel Fragments, 125

Wrede, W., 129

Zealot, Jesus as a, 136